Journeys Into Mark

16 Lessons of Exploration and Discovery

Raymond Apicella

Nihil Obstat: Rev. Hilarion Kistner, O.F.M.
Rev. Christopher R. Armstrong

Imprimi Potest: Rev. Jeremy Harrington, O.F.M.
Provincial

Imprimatur: +James H. Garland, V.G.
Archdiocese of Cincinnati
May 18, 1989

The *nihil obstat* and *imprimatur* are a declaration that a book is considered to be free from doctrinal or moral error. It is not implied that those who have granted the *nihil obstat* and *imprimatur* agree with the contents, opinions or statements expressed.

Book design and cover illustration by Julie Lonneman

ISBN 0-86716-112-4

Acknowledgments

A number of people were key to my completing this project and are deserving of recognition. Dr. Patricia O'Connor, St. Edward's University in Austin, Texas, patiently critiqued my writing for each of the 16 Journeys. Additional editing and encouragement was provided by Mary Reed Newland and Sister Joan Chittister. Special thanks is due to Angie Santasieri, Mary and Craig Carter Waren, Rick Williams and Sister Susan McGillicuddy who participated as my sample population to critique my manual. Thanks is also due to Dr. Cynthia Campbell, Dr. Lewis Donelson and Dr. Ralph Underwood from the Austin Presbyterian Theological Seminary who guided me through completion of this project, which was a portion of a larger document written to satisfy requirements for a doctorate in ministry. Deserving of my deepest gratitude are Dr. Joseph Iannone and Dr. Mercedes Iannone who acted as consultants. It was their love, concern and encouragement, along with their probing and questioning, that assisted in making this paper more than it otherwise would have been.

From a personal standpoint, I am grateful to two individuals: Joseph Ruperto and Elizabeth Jackson. Throughout the time that I was writing this manual, Joe struggled with cancer. It was Joe's dealing with life and death which enfleshed for me a deeper love of Mark's concept of the Cross. On completion of this project, it was the love of Elizabeth Jackson and her promise to be my spouse which taught me the wonder of the Resurrection.

Dedication

To all the people who have taught me the love of the Gospel and the beauty of Mark's writing.

Contents

Introduction

Journeys Into Mark derives from my teaching experiences at St. Edward's University in Austin, Texas, and at St. Thomas University in Miami. I have presented Scripture on two levels: formal undergraduate and graduate courses and adult education courses for parishes and diocesan certification programs.

The joy of presenting Scripture is knowing the marvelous effect it causes in people's lives as they gain further insight into the wonders of God presented in the Bible. These 16 Journeys are not offered as scholarly material to increase knowledge; their purpose is not to produce biblical scholars but to nourish Christians hungry to be filled with the Word of God. They are tools which allow the insights of current biblical understanding to touch your mind and heart so that you enter deeper into your relationship with God.

It is difficult to explain why I begin my scriptural sharings with Mark's Gospel. I do know that Mark's Gospel has held my attention for a long period of time. Each time I am confronted with the text, I long to learn more and more. My own journey began in a parish where I served several years ago. Each Lent Reginald Fuller, an Anglican biblical scholar from Virginia Theological Seminary, presented teachings on the Scriptures. When he shared his insights on Mark's Gospel, his excitement and enthusiasm ignited a desire within me to learn more about Mark's message. This quest continues to remain with me, and I now share the results of my own study with you.

Journeys Into Mark is presented in manual form. It encourages you to write in the book, to set your own pace for learning and to continue to build your understanding of the Gospel. Each Journey offers background information (Exploring), reflective exercises (Discoveries) and points for review (Looking Back), as well as a list of resources for further study (Exploring Further). Within each Journey, you will be asked to write impressions, ideas or insights as a start to the learning experience. The diverse responses one can make in the exercises will become the basis for discussion throughout a particular Journey.

There is no risk regarding the time and effort you spend on each Journey. Because the manual is self-paced, you may spend as much time with Mark as you desire. Only two exercises, Journey 1 and Journey 16, should be completed in one sitting. Places to break are marked in the other Journeys.

Although the manual is designed for individuals to use alone, it can be adapted by small groups for communal Bible study. Used for group learning, the manual provides rich opportunities for sharing and discussion of material.

Before Your Journey

Mark's Gospel, although presumably written in colloquial Greek, is a haunting message of our continuous relationship with God as presented by Jesus, the Christ. Mark wrote around the year A.D. 70, a time of great political unrest, as you will discover in Journey 12. The area we know as the Holy Land had been under Roman domination for over 130 years. From A.D. 66, several groups, especially zealots, attempted to overthrow the Roman government. Finally, when these rebellious groups had worn down the patience of the Romans, the government retaliated with the destruction of Jerusalem.

Among the anti-Roman government groups affected by the chaotic political situation was a cluster of individuals who had referred to themselves as "Followers of the Way" or "Christians" since the Ascension of Jesus and who had been waiting for the Messiah to return in glory. Having believed the end was near, now the glory of the Kingdom of God seemed dashed by Roman domination. Mark writes his Gospel to offer hope amidst their despair. He does not want his community to forget the mission given them by Christ—a mission of servanthood. Mark sees the chaos of the times as the foundation on which to build his community's understanding of the meaning of the cross.

Although biblical scholars are not certain of the makeup of the Marcan community, they assume a number of things. Mark's emphasis on the cross challenges his community to grasp the Christian understanding of Christ's passion in a time of persecution. Scholars also believe Mark was writing to a predominantly Gentile community since he explains Jewish celebrations that were familiar to a Jewish community. Evidence of this appears in his explanation of the slaughter of the Passover lambs on the first day of Unleavened Bread (Mark 14:12) and his explanation that the Preparation Day is the day before the sabbath (Mark 15:42). Mark also translates Aramaic words unfamiliar to a Gentile community: *Golgotha* is translated "Skull Place" (Mark 15:22) and "*Eloi.*"

Two locations are suggested as the home of Mark's community: Syria and Rome. Large settlements of Christians were found in both areas. Persecution of

Christians was occurring in both places. Those favoring a Roman location note that the Marcan community may have been distressed over the martyrdoms of Paul and Peter. Rome, as a cosmopolitan town of trade and commerce, allowed for the easy spread of the Gospel throughout the known world. On the other hand, Syria's Eastern location finds favor because of the community's strong mixture of both Jewish and Gentile influences. Like the Roman location, Syria also is believed to have been a cosmopolitan area at the time.

Just as scholars provide educated guesses regarding the Marcan community, they propose various theories regarding the author. Nowhere in the Gospel is the author identified. A second-century tradition, however, has attributed this Gospel to the man Mark. Mark was believed to be a disciple of Peter who recorded Peter's remembrance of Christ. The objection to this Peter-Mark connection is set forth in the question: Why aren't the writings entitled "Gospel of Peter" since Peter is a more prominent figure than Mark?

References to a "John Mark" appear in other sections of the Christian Scriptures (New Testament). The Book of Acts speaks of the home of Mary, mother of John Mark, as a favorite gathering place for Christians (Acts 12:12). Mark was taken on the first missionary journey of Paul and Barnabas, Mark's cousin. He is mentioned in numerous Pauline documents (Philemon 24; Colossians 4:10; 2 Timothy 4:11) and in 1 Peter 5:13. In the end, however, there is no conclusive evidence for the identity of the author.

Despite the failure to discover the true identity of the author, we are assured that he was a believer in Christ's message, respected by the Christian community and, more importantly, filled with the desire to reveal the true identity of Jesus for his own community and for Christian communities of all time.

Mark's fervor to reveal Christ, not himself, is displayed in these Journeys. Despite the chaos of the times, Mark provides an authentic image of Christ which offers hope and salvation to a community struggling to understand their times and their life. It is precisely this presentation of the authentic image of Jesus which moves us to call Mark's writings the "Good News."

Journey 1

Beginning Anew

Mark's Gospel was meant to be heard rather than read. The initial writing was prepared on long scrolls of papyrus without any division of chapter and verse. The early writer of the Gospel (the storyteller) longs for the listener to proclaim, "Jesus is the Son of God," at the story's conclusion.

Today there are endless copies of Mark's Gospel. People have Bibles in their homes, discover Bibles in hotel rooms or have Bibles distributed to them at churches, airports or by door-to-door evangelists. Bible passages are read in Sunday services, and some churches provide copies of passages for reading along with the minister or priest.

Although the easy availability of Bibles may seem an advantage, the disadvantage is that often when people are so inundated with the written word they are unable to *listen* to *the Word*. Unfortunately, when individuals know the characters, know the plot and know the ending, they often fool themselves into believing they know the story. My own inability to "know the story" is revealed in the many Sundays when I have left my parish church without remembering what the Gospel reading was for the day.

The challenge of Journey 1 is to hear the story *anew*. This is possible if you envision yourself as a first-century Christian listening to Mark's rendition of Jesus' life and experiencing your faith beginnings. To accomplish this, first try to block from your mind previous encounters you had with the Gospel of Mark, whether from homilies or classes.

Second, do not assume you know the Gospel story even though it has been previously read to you or you have read it yourself. Rather, force yourself to complete the entire reading.

Third, through the use of imagination, pretend you are a first-century person listening to Mark telling you this story of Jesus.

Finally, train your ears to hear the story as if listening for the first time and attempting to ignite your heart with the beauty of the story. These suggestions will allow you to *hear* the story *anew*, so that your heart will be set on fire with the love of Jesus and enable you to proclaim with other believers: "Jesus is the Son of God."

Discovering

For this first exercise you are asked to read Mark's Gospel in one sitting. It will take about one hour and 45 minutes. Time is not the issue here; the challenge is not to match the estimated time but to hear the story anew. A few techniques may assist you in listening to the story:

- Provide yourself the luxury of a quiet place and time to accomplish this task.
- Move your lips while reading, or read the Gospel aloud to yourself.
- Small groups should select one member to act as reader while the others listen.

While reading, the "hearer" should be listening for key words, phrases and ideas repeated throughout the Gospel. After "hearing" Mark's story of Jesus, you should write these key words, phrases and ideas in the space provided as part of the exercise. After reading the Gospel you will be asked: Who do you think Jesus is for Mark? You may want to keep this question in mind while reading.

For now, open your Bible to Mark's Gospel and begin *listening* to his story of Jesus. Be sure to read all of Mark's Gospel.

Discovering

In the space provided write the key words, phrases and ideas you heard while listening to Mark's Gospel. *Remember, there is a diversity of responses.* As words, phrases and ideas come to consciousness, simply list them. Try to list three to 10 things.

1)

2)

3)

4)

5)

6)

7)

8)

9)

10)

Discovering

In the space provided write one or two sentences responding to the question: Who is Jesus for Mark?

Discovering

Now that you have read the Gospel of Mark, list questions regarding the Gospel that you hope this book will answer:

Exploring: Key Words in Mark's Gospel

You now have compiled a listing of key words, phrases and ideas, as well as particular questions, from listening to Mark's Gospel. Next is a listing of key words, phrases and ideas I have heard from my reading. You may want to compare the two listings since this exercise will become the central focus of our Journeys into Mark's Gospel.

The key words, phrases and ideas I have heard in Mark's Gospel are:

1) Repeated use of the word *immediately* creates a sense of urgency.

2) When Jesus performs a miracle, he instructs the person *not to say anything*.

3) Jesus' words and actions are a source of *amazement* for people.

4) Jesus has power over *demons and evil spirits*.

5) Jesus mentions that he is going to Jerusalem to *suffer and die*.

6) Jesus has the *power* to heal the sick and the infirm.

7) The disciples (especially Peter) *do not always understand* what Jesus is saying.

8) Mark frequently uses the titles *Son of God* and *Son of Man*.

9) Peter (at Caesarea Philippi) and the centurion (at the foot of the cross) recognize Jesus as *the anointed one* (Messiah) and *Son of God*.

10) The ending of the Gospel is abrupt. The women *flee from the tomb* "bewildered and trembling; and because of their great fear, they said nothing to anyone" (Mark 16:8).*

In upcoming Journeys we will discuss some of these key words, phrases and ideas. Through these explanations, I hope some of your questions will be answered.

Looking back

On Journey 1 you made the following discoveries:

• the importance of reading the Gospel in one sitting;
• techniques for hearing the Gospel;
• the importance of listening for key ideas, words and phrases in the Gospel.

For Further Exploration

Rhoads, David and Donald Michie. *Mark as Story: An Introduction to the Narrative of a Gospel.* Philadelphia: Fortress Press, 1982.

---

* In Gospel citations the first number refers to the *chapter*, which is followed by a *colon*, and the next number lists the *verse or verses*. For example, Mark 1:1 is the first chapter, first verse of the Gospel.

Journey 2
The First Verse

Every story has a title, either stated or implied. Often we know a story from its title, such as *Cinderella* or *Alice in Wonderland*. Or we begin our personal stories with an implied title: "Did I tell you the story of the day my car broke down on the freeway?" Story titles try in a few words to hint at the story's plot. A story title suggests a story with a beginning, a middle and an end. Although many of us refer to Mark's story as "The Gospel of St. Mark," or simply, "Mark's Gospel," scholars believe that Mark's real title is presented in the first verse of his first chapter.

Discovering

In the translation I am using, Mark 1:1 reads:

> Here begins the gospel of Jesus Christ, the Son of God.

In the space provided formulate your understanding of each word in Mark's title. While working with words in the title, exclude articles and prepositions; however, consider *Jesus* and *Christ* as separate words but *Son of God* as one word.

1)

2)

3)

4)

5)

6)

Exploring: Key Words in the First Verse

The following is my list of the six key words in the title of Mark's Gospel. (It should be noted that we are working with an English translation of this passage. In the original Greek translation, we do not find the verb *begins* or the adverb *here*.)

Here. Used as an adverb, the word *here* implies "in this place" or "at the present moment" or "in this world." Mark captures your attention with the word *here* by telling you it is in this present moment and within this world that his story begins.

Begins. The *present tense* verb of the title also captures the immediacy of the action. This story is not about the past ("began") or the future ("will begin") but the present moment. The use of present-tense verbs is a technique found frequently in Mark's writing: He includes 151 present-tense verbs within his Gospel. This writing technique places you within the story and sets such a rapid pace that you may experience a feeling of urgency or "gasping for breath" similar to running a race.

Gospel. Gospel means "good news," and, indeed, Mark's Gospel is good news. The word *gospel* may be traced to a secular meaning: Caesar Augustus' birthday was proclaimed as the beginning of the new year and as "good news" for the entire world.

In the Hebrew Scriptures (Old Testament) the idea of "good news" is when a messenger announces Israel's redemption from exile. An example of this understanding of "good news" is found in Isaiah 52:7-10. Although we do not have the word *gospel* within this Old Testament citation, we do have a backdrop for understanding what is meant when "good news" is proclaimed:

> How beautiful upon the mountains
> are the feet of him who brings glad tidings,
> Announcing peace, bearing good news,
> announcing salvation, and saying to Zion,
> "Your God is King!"

In Mark the term gospel (*evangelion* in Greek) refers to the Good News preached by Jesus that the Kingdom of God is at hand.

Jesus. This is the *name* for Jesus rather than a title for him. Just as our names may mean something else (Raymond means protector), the name Jesus means "savior" or "salvation is here" or, more accurately, "Yahweh saves."

Christ. This is a common *title* often joined to Jesus' name: The term *Christ* means "anointed one."

Son of God. At first glance this title suggests that Jesus is the biological son of the Father. The problem with this notion is the implication that the Father existed first and that somewhere in time and history the Son was created. Our belief in the Trinity claims that both Son and Father (as well as Spirit) always were, always are and always will be.

"Son of God" can mean many things. Mark selects particular meaning for this expression. In his title the expression is creedal (a faith statement); it professes that Jesus is uniquely related to God, totally immersed in God and in doing God's work. It is Mark's intention to clarify this title and the relationship between Jesus and God throughout his Gospel. Because two titles—*Son of God* and *Son of Man*—are crucial to Mark's Gospel, you will have an opportunity to deal with these terms in a future Journey.

Mark's use of various titles for Jesus at the beginning of his Gospel reveals something about who this Jesus is for Mark and for the listener. Jesus is savior, anointed one and one like God. Very cleverly, Mark is introducing us to his Christology, that is, an articulation of who Jesus the Christ is for Mark and his community.

Looking Back

On Journey 2 you made the following discoveries:

- Mark 1:1 is the title of the Gospel.
- Gospel means "good news."
- Mark's Gospel places the reader within the action.
- The terms *Jesus, Christ* and *Son of God* reveal Mark's understanding of who Jesus is for him and his community.

For Further Exploration

Flanagan, Neal. *Mark, Matthew, and Luke: A Guide to the Gospel Parallels.* Collegeville, Minn.: The Liturgical Press, 1978.

Spivey, Robert and D. Moody Smith. *Anatomy of the New Testament: A Guide to Its Structure and Meaning,* 3rd ed. New York: Macmillan Publishing Co., 1982.

Journey 3

The Decision for the Contemporary Explorer

Do you want to know what Jesus said, or do you want to know *Jesus* through what he is saying? Does the first part of this question sound theoretical and critical and the second part elementary and superficial?

Yet how critically correct is it to learn "all about" a person and never "know" the person himself or herself? This is why Mark places on the lips of Jesus, "Let the children come to me and do not hinder them. It is to just such as these that the kingdom of God belongs" (Mark 10:14).

What Mark suggests in this passage is that we stop trying to pretend "we have it all together" (No one really does!), and be open, trusting and spontaneous like children in expressing honestly our feelings, doubts and joys. This gut-level learning will allow us to develop new concepts and avoid believing we are someone because "we have all the facts."

Samuel Taylor Coleridge, the 19th-century poet and theologian, referred to this as "a willing suspension of disbelief." For example, only after a play or movie has ended can you analyze and evaluate the truth, goodness, beauty and practicality of what you have experienced.

The beginning Journeys into Mark's Gospel should be like this. Let the Gospel's feelings touch you first, then analyze and evaluate the history and literary forms and, finally, draw your own conclusions.

The following reflective exercises are designed to assist you in knowing Jesus and knowing yourself. Through a series of reflections on Mark's Gospel, I hope you can discover the true meaning of this Journey and find an opportunity to speak to Jesus in an open and trusting fashion expressing your personal doubts, fears and joys.

Discovering

This exercise will provide a technique for reflecting on Jesus in Mark's Gospel. Read through the entire exercise first, then return to step 1 and follow each step to its conclusion.

1) Find a place where you can be alone to read and reflect quietly for about 45 minutes.

2) Reduce the tension throughout your body by concentrating on each of your body parts in turn, starting with the soles of your feet and moving upward—feet, legs,

torso, arms, shoulders, neck—until you reach the top of your head. As you concentrate on each part of your body, place that portion of your body in a state of relaxation. Say simply: "I cast all tension and anxiety out of my _____ and replace that tension with the peace of Christ."

3) Place your Bible on your lap, close your eyes and imagine that you are a person in first-century Galilee. To assist you with this image, visualize the countryside of Galilee, the physical characteristics of people from this village, their type of dress, what Jesus looks like, the sounds and smells surrounding you in this picture.

Then imagine that you have heard about this new wandering prophet, Jesus of Nazareth, and you want to see if he really has some wisdom to share with you. Invite Jesus to a place where it is most comfortable for the two of you to talk alone: the seashore, a field, a forest, a mountaintop or a candlelight supper.

4) Ask Jesus, "How can I be a happier person?" Open your Bible and slowly read Mark 12:28-31. Reflect on the answer presented in the passage and allow the words to become a part of you.

5) Ask Jesus, "Why do you want me to love my enemies?" Read and reflect on Mark 11:25.

6) Ask Jesus, "Why is it so difficult to pray at times?" Read and reflect on Mark 11:22-24.

7) Ask Jesus, "How can I be true to my own values and enjoy personal integrity without being a hypocrite?" Read and reflect on Mark 12:41-44.

8) Ask Jesus, "Just between us, who are you really?" Read and reflect on Mark 1:7-8.

9) Ask Jesus, "If I want to become your disciple, what would I have to do?" Read and reflect on Mark 8:34-35.

In the space provided summarize what Jesus said in answer to each of your six questions.

1) How can I be a happier person?

2) Why do you want me to love my enemies?

3) Why is it so hard to pray sometimes?

4) How can I be true to my own values and enjoy personal integrity?

5) Just between us, who are you really?

6) What should I do to become your disciple?

Looking Back

On Journey 3 you made the following discoveries:

- Reflective exercises may aid you in truly knowing a Gospel.
- Various techniques for reflective exercises may be used as tools for imagining Gospel accounts.
- Writing your reflections may help you become a contemporary explorer.

Journey 4

Everyone Has a Plan

We begin many of life's tasks with a plan, from the simple preparation of the weekly supermarket shopping list to the serious contemplation of what we will do with the rest of our lives. At times, the plan changes in midstream: The bakery item not on the shopping list proves too luscious to pass by or a serious illness changes the course of our life.

The Gospel writers also have a plan. Their main intention is to reveal Christ to believing communities. Journey 4 will help you discover Mark's Gospel plan. The first exercise works with nonbiblical material; the second exercise applies the learning to the Marcan Gospel.

Discovering: Journey in 2987

The year is A.D. 2987. You are part of a group of people who do not speak English and who take all meals in pill form. With friends, you are on an archaeological expedition in Austin, Texas—a place where you know signs of ancient human life have often been found. Your group intends to publish a book based on your finds. During the trip, a member discovers a small fragment of paper which looks like this:

"Please pass the salt

What does this message reveal about this ancient people? From this message alone, what words, ideas and discoveries can you claim about this group of people who lived in Austin eons ago? In the space provided list at least 10 words, ideas or discoveries, or as many more ideas as come to mind. *Remember, there is a diversity of opinions.*

1)

2)

3)

4)

5)

6)

7)

8)

9)

10)

Exploring

The following is a list of the top 10 words, ideas and discoveries that I think can be claimed about this ancient group of people. Compare your list with mine.

1) The group in Austin had a language.

2) The group was an intelligent group because they had a means of written communication.

3) Through sophisticated laboratory techniques, we may be able to determine the date of this message and the composition of the paper and writing material.

4) To understand this message, we will have to study the language, the customs and culture of this ancient group.

5) The group in Austin was industrious: They could produce paper and writing instruments.

6) The message is in English: "Please pass the salt."

7) The group in Austin was a social and polite group of people as shown by their use of *please*.

8) The quotation marks in front of the word *please* indicate the words may come from a direct quote by an unknown person.

9) Their food source was different from your "pill meals" because the phrase suggests some type of food seasoning.

10) The group was communal and took meals together.

All 10 of these ideas begin with assumptions. For example, you assume the last word of the message to be *salt* because you can recognize it on paper. Your "discovery," however, may be a translation of a text rather than the original piece of work. It also is possible that during translations some scribe misspelled the word, crossing the final *l* and making *sall* look like *salt*. It is possible, too, that the word may not be "salt" at all but really *sally lunn*—a sweet bread found in the South.

If your assumptions are incorrect, the majority of your conclusions will also be incorrect. If so, your publishing plan must be reexamined and a new plan devised, one based on correct assumptions.

This simple exercise above provides you with some techniques that biblical scholars use to understand the Gospel plan. Since both the original document written by Mark and Mark himself are unavailable for examination, scholars must make assumptions in order to arrive at their theories about Mark's plan for his Gospel. These assumptions are tested and retested until a workable theory is proposed.

The word "theory" does not imply a lack of truth but rather implies the best intelligent conclusion. At the moment, we live daily by a vast number of theories: the theory of relativity, the developmental theories of psychology, medical theories about cancer and numerous health theories pertaining to jogging.

The next exercise will introduce you to the present biblical theories regarding Mark's overall plan for his Gospel. These theories have been tested and retested through a long process of biblical study by hundreds of scholars over a period of 2,000 years.

Discovering: Journey Into Heritage

In 1875 my grandfather, Vincenzo Apicella, was the last of 17 children born to a poor family who managed a small bakery in Amalfi, Italy. When he was 19 years of age, Vincenzo was instructed by his father to travel to America, make money and then send for the rest of the family. Along with a friend, Vincenzo walked from Amalfi to Naples to seek passage to the new land. Having no money, Vincenzo hid on a ship bound for America. After spending three days in hiding, he presented himself to the captain, who promptly forced Vincenzo to work in payment for passage.

Upon arrival in New York harbor, Vincenzo learned that immigrants were being detained on Ellis Island, so he jumped ship and swam to shore. Reaching the shore of the Hudson River, my grandfather was discovered by a man who told him: "If you vote Republican, I will give you a job in New Haven." My grandfather did not know what *Republican* or *New Haven* meant. He did know *job*, however, and spent the remaining days of his life in New Haven. He never returned to Amalfi nor did he acquire sufficient funds to send for his family.

My grandfather died nine months before I was born. I never knew the story of his coming to America until 1979 when, as an adult, I visited a distant relative in Amalfi. Since the relative in Amalfi was younger than I, he did not know my grandfather either. All he knew was the story. We have no way to verify whether my grandfather really was a stowaway aboard a ship, whether he swam the Hudson or whether he ever voted Republican.

I love this story of my grandfather, however, and feel closer to him than many of my other relatives. The story's importance for me is not the facts but what it reveals of my heritage.

Biblical study contains components similar to those in the story of my grandfather. Just as I do not know the *exact* conversations of my grandfather with his father, with the ship's captain or with the man on the Hudson shore, the Bible does not contain the *exact* words spoken by Jesus. Rather, the words presented in the Bible have gone through three levels:

1) what Jesus actually said;

2) what the disciples preached about Jesus and his sayings;

3) what was written about what Jesus said.

These three levels highlight the movement from oral tradition to written tradition. Certainly, Jesus spent his years of ministry training his disciples and instructing them about the Kingdom. This is level one.

After the death and resurrection of Jesus, the disciples preached the message of Jesus to their communities. The preaching was geared towards particular communities and was based on *remembrance* of Jesus' words, not his exact words. This is level two.

Finally, a writer such as Mark saves the stories and preachings in written form. This is level three.

Just as I have related a story about my grandfather which occurred almost a century ago, Mark relates the faith story of Jesus which happened approximately 40 years before the actual writing. Assuming a date of writing of around A.D. 70 for Mark's Gospel and placing Jesus' death in our calendar year of A.D. 33, there is a span of 37 years before Mark begins his writing. Mark's plan takes the stories of Jesus and places them in a particular arrangement to say something specific to his particular community. Mark's plan is to arrange the story of Jesus to inspire his readers to believe in the Christ.

Your previous work with nonbiblical material and your understanding of the movement from the oral to the written tradition allow you to begin working with Mark's structural plan for his Gospel. That structure will be revealed in the following exercise.

In the space provided, write the following verses from Mark's Gospel:

1:1

8:29 (only what Peter says)

8:31 (the first 14 words)

15:39 (what the Centurion says)

Exploring

The scriptural passages you have written are the framework of Mark's structural plan. The first half of the Gospel is 1:1 to 8:30; the second half of the Gospel is 8:31 to 15:39.

Two major parts of Mark's Gospel answer two questions. In the following chart you will find these questions and the scriptural citations which answer them.

Question: Who is this man, Jesus?
Answer: The Messiah (8:29).

Question: What kind of Messiah is he?
Answer: The Son of God (15:39).

Discovering

It would be wise to pause in prayer at this point. Refer to the points for reflective exercises in Journey 3. In reflecting on the material in this Journey, ask yourself the same questions Mark presents to his community:

• Who is this man Jesus for me?
• What kind of Messiah is Jesus for me?
• What does it mean to me that Jesus is the suffering Son of Man and Son of God?

Looking Back

On Journey 4 you made the following discoveries:

- an appreciation for biblical study through the use of nonbiblical material;
- an understanding of "theory" in modern biblical study;
- the movement from oral to written tradition;
- the overall structure of Mark's Gospel, answering the questions, "Who is this man?" and "What type of Messiah is he?";
- additional material for reflective exercises.

For Further Exploration

Kelber, Werner. *The Oral and the Written Gospel*. Philadelphia: Fortress Press, 1983.

Senior, Donald and Eugene LaVerdiere. *Gospel of Mark*, Audiocassettes 1-4. Austin, Texas: Texas Catholic Conference Scripture Seminar, 1984.

Journey 5
Mark's Plan for You to Follow

The previous Journey introduced you to the overall structural plan of Mark's Gospel. You discovered Mark's Gospel is divided into two major parts and answers two important questions: Who is this man? What kind of Messiah is he? As the Preface and Journey 1 state, Mark's purpose for writing his Gospel is to reveal Jesus to the reader/listener. Besides revealing Christ, Mark's writings also will reveal something about you as a follower of Christ.

As a fine piece of literature captures your attention because it rings true to life, Mark's Gospel challenges you to grasp the elements of the true Christian life. You are encouraged to put yourself in the place of the characters in the story, a literary device referred to as "mimetic."

In Journey 4 you were introduced to the mimetic device when you were asked to reflect on your responses to the questions: What kind of man? What kind of Messiah? Here the mimetic device asks you to put yourself in the place of Peter and/or the Centurion and to proclaim as your own the statements: "You are the Messiah!" (8:29) and "Clearly this man is the Son of God!" (15:39).

Using the mimetic device with Mark's Gospel helps you to paint a picture of the Christian life. This method draws your attention to various characters as models of the Christian life-style and encourages you to substitute yourself for the character in the scene, to become the character.

This exercise helps you acquire a broad overview of Mark's understanding of the Christian life by employing the mimetic device to the characters of John the Baptist, Jesus and the disciples.

Discovering: John the Baptist

Read Mark 1:6-7.

Who is the main character of these verses?

In one word, what is the major action of this character?

Read Mark 1:14a (the first part of the verse).*

What happens to the main character in 1:14a?

Read Mark 6:28.

What has happened to the main character?

Discovering: Jesus

Read Mark 1:14b (the second part of the verse).

Who is the main character of this verse?

What is the major action of this character?

Read Mark 8:31.

What is going to happen to this character?

---

* Bible verses are often divided into two parts, *a* and *b*, with *a* designating the first part of the verse and *b* designating the second part of the verse. For example, 1:14a refers to the first chapter, the first part of the 14th verse.

Read Mark 15:37.

What has happened to this character?

Discovering: Disciples

Read Mark 1:16-18.

What is the action of these characters after they are called by Jesus?

Read Mark 13:10.

What is the action required of the characters in this verse?

Read Mark 13:13.

What are the consequences of this action?

Discovering

Refer to the work you have just completed concerning John, Jesus and the disciples. In studying your answers, do you recognize any pattern that Mark is presenting? In the space provided write a summary of Mark's pattern which you may have discovered using the mimetic device in the scriptural passages regarding John, Jesus and the disciples.

Exploring

You now have discovered Mark's idea of what it means to be a follower of Jesus. You also may have discovered a certain pattern developing:

- John preached (1:7); John is arrested (1:14); John is killed (6:28).
- Jesus preached (1:14); Jesus is going to be arrested and persecuted (8:31); Jesus is killed (15:37).
- The disciples are called to preach (1:16-18); the disciples preach the Good News (13:10); the disciples will be arrested (13:9); the Book of Acts and tradition tell us that many of the disciples were killed.

If you have employed the mimetic device, you have "become" John the Baptist, Jesus and the disciples. As each of them, you fit in this shocking picture by realizing that if you preach the Gospel, you will be arrested, and eventually you must be prepared to die. Your proclamation was stated in the first verse of the Gospel: "Here begins the gospel of Jesus Christ, the Son of God" (1:1). To make this statement and pronounce this creed will lead you along the same path as John, Jesus and the disciples.

With further discovery, you will note the rapid pace of Mark's writing. Refer to 1:14. In the first part of the verse John is arrested (1:14a); in the second part Jesus immediately assumes John's position (1:14b). This writing style, with the frequent use of present tense verbs, provides an additional example of the Gospel's rapid pace.

You will find additional insight into Mark's writing style by reading 6:7-30. In these verses, you can imagine Mark's presentation as three scenes from a play. In scene one, the disciples are sent off to preach the need for repentance. The audience is left with an empty stage. In order to fill the empty stage, Mark presents a second scene, the death of John the Baptist. Once you have been informed of what has happened to John, scene two is finished. The disciples return (6:30), and now you begin scene three. To continue his rapid pace, Mark presents action after action after action.

Looking Back

On Journey 5, you made the following discoveries:

- The mimetic device allows you to move into the Gospel writings. You substitute yourself for major characters and recognize the similarity between their response to Jesus and your response to Jesus.
- The call of the Christian is to follow the life of Jesus, which is one of preaching the Word, willingness to suffer and possible physical death.
- Mark's Gospel presents various scenes in the life of the disciples. These scenes give us another example of Mark's proclivity for constant action.

For Further Exploration

Flanagan, Neal. *Mark, Matthew, and Luke: A Guide to the Gospel Parallels.* Collegeville, Minn.: The Liturgical Press, 1978.

Journey 6
Enter Into the Specifics

The first five Journeys have presented broad overviews of Mark's Gospel. By now you have become familiar with Mark's structural division by answering the questions, "Who is this man?" and "What kind of Messiah is he?" You also have investigated the mimetic device—the technique for putting yourself within the Gospel—and have reflected on the creedal statement presented in 1:1.

To deepen your understanding of Mark's picture of Jesus, the Christ, you must now explore some characteristic aspects of Mark's Gospel. Journey 6 encourages you to work with specific Marcan passages, to dig deeper into this marvelous message.

Discovering

In this exercise you are asked to read a particular passage and immediately write a summary of what the passage contains. For example, for Mark 1:1, you would write "a creedal statement proclaiming Jesus to be the Son of God."

Read the following verses and then write a word, phrase or sentence that comes to consciousness after reading the verse.

Mark 1:10-11

Mark 1:23-26

Mark 1:34

Mark 3:11-12

Mark 5:6-10

Can you summarize a common thread found in each of these five passages?

Exploring

In the five passages above, did you find the common element to be proclaiming Jesus as the Son of God or as one who has authority over evil spirits? Mark creates a pattern in which Jesus is recognized as the Son of God. If you reflect on all of the passages presented for this exercise (including 1:1), you may discover the following:

• The reader (you) makes a profession of faith that Jesus is the Son of God.
• At the baptism of Jesus it is revealed (unveiled) that he is the "beloved Son." Jesus sees "the sky rent in two and the Spirit descending on him like a dove" (1:10-11).
• The unclean spirit recognizes Jesus as "the holy One of God" (1:24). Jesus silences him and casts him out of the demoniac.
• Jesus expels many demons (1:34) but does not permit them to speak.
• Again, unclean spirits catch sight of Jesus (3:11) and shout, "You are the Son of God!" Again, Jesus instructs the unclean spirits not to reveal his identity.
• In the final passage the legion of unclean spirits refers to Jesus as "Son of God Most High" (5:7).

These passages suggest that the true identity of Jesus is known by only a few. The most obvious "knowers" are the unclean spirits. In four of the six passages, they proclaim Jesus as Son of God, Holy One and Most High. They are able to see something in Jesus that many others are not able to see. Why does Jesus command the unclean spirits to be silent about this revelation? This element of silence or secrecy will be discussed in Journey 10.

At the baptism of Jesus, there is a revelation to Jesus that he is the "beloved Son." Careful reading of 1:10-11 indicates that this revelation is to Jesus alone. The message is given to Jesus and not to the crowd watching. In 1:10-11, Mark writes: "On coming up out of the water *he* [emphasis added] saw....'*You* [emphasis added] are my beloved....' " This revelation to Jesus that he is the "beloved Son" presents two difficult questions.

The first question forces us to investigate what Mark means by the "Son of God." The second question asks when did Jesus realize that he was the "Son of God." The answer to the former question will unfold as you continue your study of Mark. The answers to the latter question are many, and you are free to select any one of the responses listed next.

- Jesus always knew he was the Son of God.
- Jesus became aware that he was the Son of God at his baptism.
- Jesus became aware that he was the Son of God during the Agony in the Garden.
- Jesus became aware he was the Son of God on the cross or at the time of death.

Reflection on *all* of the passages reveals deeper insight into Mark's writing. Thus far, three groups or individuals are aware of the power of Jesus: (1) the reader or people of faith, including Mark and his community (assumed from the reflection on 1:1); (2) the unclean spirits who are fearful of the authority of Jesus; and (3) Jesus himself, through the private revelation given to him at the baptism.

Discovering: The Bystanders

But what about the other characters in the Gospel and their understanding of who Jesus really is? To capture an understanding of these other characters, you will be asked again to read and write the word, phrase or sentence which comes to mind after reading.

Mark 1:22

Mark 1:27

Mark 6:2

Summarize people's reactions to Jesus from these three passages.

Exploring

Notice in these three accounts that the people are *spellbound* (1:22) and *amazed* (1:27, 6:2). Their amazement comes from witnessing the authority by which Jesus teaches. His teaching is different from that of other teachers. His authority is evident in both his words and his deeds. His words cause *amazement*; his expulsion of unclean spirits and his healings cause *amazement*.

Through this group of people, Mark tells us that the hearers of Jesus recognize his authority but, because they do not fully grasp its meaning, they are *amazed*.

Discovering: The Religious Leaders

Amazement and authority now take on a different meaning for other characters in Mark's Gospel. Again you are asked to read and to write your impressions of the following passages:

Mark 2:6

Mark 3:21

Mark 3:22

Mark 8:11

Summarize the common characteristics of this group of people.

This group lacks an understanding of who Jesus really is. Here are accounts of some scribes and Pharisees (religious leaders of the time who should know better) who either question Jesus or accuse him of blasphemy. There is also an account of Jesus' family's belief that he is out of his mind (3:21).

Discovering: The Disciples

One may wonder about the disciples of Jesus during this time. What were their reactions to this Jesus? The following passages shed light on Jesus' disciples. Read the passages and write your brief impressions.

Mark 4:13

Mark 4:40

Mark 6:51-52

Summarize your discovery regarding the disciples and their understanding of Jesus.

Discovering: The Believers

Finally, there is a group of people who understand Jesus more obviously than others.

Read and summarize your understanding of the following four passages:

Mark 1:40-41; 2:5; 5:20; 5:28-34

Exploring

In studying the passages regarding the disciples, you will find the disciples similar to the first group of people, the bystanders. They also are amazed, but they seemingly do not understand. The disciples are filled with fear and even after witnessing the actions of Jesus still do not comprehend the full meaning of his message.

Finally, the last group of people—the leper (1:40), the paralytic (2:5), the people of Decapolis (5:20) and the woman sick for 12 years (5:28)—are open to belief in Jesus.

Again, employ the mimetic device and place yourself in any one of these stories. You may see yourself as a person of faith and open to belief, or you may be confused, questioning, even disbelieving. Each role will offer new insight into the Scripture passages.

Looking Back

On Journey 6 you made the following discoveries:

- Jesus' baptism is a private revelation to him alone.
- In addition to Jesus, the reader (you, Mark and his community) and the evil spirits are aware of who Jesus really is.
- Despite Mark's emphasis on Jesus as the Son of God, the disciples do not have a clear understanding of Jesus' identity.
- The authorities (Pharisees and scribes) should recognize Jesus but not all do.
- Those whom Jesus heals (leper, paralytic) recognize something unique and special about Jesus.

For Further Exploration

Harrington, Wilfrid. *Mark*. New Testament Message, Vol.
    4. Wilmington, Del.: Michael Glazier, Inc., 1979.

Journey 7

Specific Techniques in Mark's Writing

Some people's eating habits may cause extreme discomfort to their family or friends. My nephew Robert often has sent his four brothers running from the kitchen table because of his spaghetti sandwiches. As a peanut butter lover, I have revolted an occasional onlooker by piling gobs of peanut butter with pickles, bacon, bananas or bologna.

Mark's writing style creates odd literary sandwiches by arranging material in just as strange a manner, but his genius allows his extraordinary arrangements to come together as a complete unit. This arrangement of disconnected materials forming an eventual unit is referred to as the "Marcan sandwich." The following exercise will introduce us to one of Mark's famous sandwich combinations.

Discovering

Read Mark 3:20-35.

Then reread the passage section by section as cited below and summarize each in the space provided.

Mark 3:20-21

Mark 3:22a

Mark 3:22b

Mark 3:23-26

Mark 3:27

Mark 3:28-29

Mark 3:31-35

Exploring

Let us compare our observations concerning Jesus' family and evil spirits. I have emphasized the pattern developing in the Marcan sandwich by repeating letters with each of my summary statements.

3:20-21: The family of Jesus come to get him, thinking he is crazy (a).

3:22a: The scribes accuse Jesus of being possessed by Beelzebul (b).

3:22b: The scribes accuse Jesus of expelling demons with the help of the prince of demons (c).

3:23-26: This is referred to as a "logion" or "teaching." In this case, it is a teaching about the false kingdom of Satan (d).

3:27: Now Jesus is ready to respond to the second accusation of cooperating with the prince of demons (c).

3:28-30: Now Jesus is ready to respond to the first accusation of being possessed by Beelzebul (b).

3:31-35: Jesus responds with a statement as to who are his true relatives (a).

The diagram which follows is another way of expressing the Marcan sandwich as a writing technique. Notice the outer layers (1), the second concern and response (2) and the "meat" of the matter at the center (3):

1) first accusation
2) second accusation
3) logion or teaching
2) response to second accusation
1) response to first accusation

Both Journey 6 and Journey 7 contain references to unclean or evil spirits. In Journey 6 the unclean spirits possess particular individuals (demoniac, 1:23-28). For Mark and his community, "demonic possession" was what people today might call mental illness, or even epilepsy.

In Journey 7 there is reference to Beelzebul and the prince of demons. The name Beelzebul derives from the name of a god of the Canaanites, neighbors of the Israelites in the Hebrew Scriptures.

In the Christian Scriptures *Beelzebul* is a reference to evil spirits. The "prince of demons" found in verse 3:22b is Satan, the leader of all the unclean or evil spirits. Thus, in the passages just studied, Jesus is first accused of possession by an unclean spirit (Beelzebul) and then later accused of being a pawn of the prince of demons (Satan).

Further clarification is also needed concerning Jesus and his relatives (3:20). The original Greek phrase *hoi par' autou* can be translated "brothers," "friends," "cousins" or "family." The term *brothers* suggests that Jesus was not an only child, a point confusing for many Roman Catholics. The Christian denominations hold three different interpretations of the term *brother.*

- Roman Catholics, rather than assume that *hoi par' autou* means "blood brother," prefer to translate it as "cousins" or "family relatives," thus maintaining belief that Jesus was an only child.
- Greek Orthodox scholars suggest that Joseph was previously married and widowed before marrying Mary. The results of his marriage to Mary produced no other children. To them, therefore, the term *brothers* means "stepbrothers."
- Some Protestant denominations suggest that Mary and Joseph had other children after Jesus and that these members mentioned in the Gospels are "blood brothers."

Mark (unlike Matthew and Luke) shows no concern for the virginal birth. Again, in 6:3, Jesus is called the son of Mary and a *brother* to James and Joses and Judas and Simon. Also in 6:3 is the question, "Are not his *sisters* our neighbors here?" (emphasis added).

The literal interpretation of *brother* or *sister* need not be a concern at this point. The deeper theological issue is that Mark is reminding us that the *true* followers of Jesus are the ones who accept the ministry of Jesus and gather about him in faith and discipleship. Important relationships to Jesus are not through kinship but rather through faith.

You may want to spend time working with additional Marcan sandwiches from the following passages: 5:25-43; 6:7-32; 11:12-25; 14:1-11.

Discovering

In addition to the "Marcan sandwich," other writing techniques also provide insight into Mark's message. The following exercise allows a deeper understanding of Jesus' relationship with his disciples. Read each section separately, summarize the passage and then compare the three sections.

Section One

a) Mark 8:30-32a

b) Mark 8:32b-33

c) Mark 8:34-35

Section Two

a) Mark 9:31

b) Mark 9:33-34

c) Mark 9:35

Section Three

a) Mark 10:32-34

b) Mark 10:35-39

c) Mark 10:42-46

Refer to the summaries you just wrote for each *a* reading. Summarize in one sentence what is happening in each of these three accounts.

a)

Refer to the summaries just written for each *b* reading. Summarize in one sentence what is happening in each of these three accounts.

b)

Finally, refer to the summaries written for each *c* account and write one sentence which summarizes the three accounts.

c)

This exercise of reading each account, summarizing the readings and then comparing the summaries is designed to allow you to see a particular pattern. Did you notice that all of the *a* accounts deal with a *prediction* of Jesus' death, all of the *b* accounts deal with a *misunderstanding* by the disciples and all *c* accounts deal with a *teaching* given to us by Jesus concerning what it means to be a true disciple?

Mark has cleverly constructed a pattern of prediction, misunderstanding and teaching. He uses this pattern three times. In addition to being a clever writer, Mark is an excellent teacher who realizes that repetition is often the key to understanding for his students.

From Journey 6 remember that the disciples, although amazed at Jesus' words and deeds, did not always understand them. Mark highlights their confusion again in this threefold pattern of prediction, misunderstanding

and teaching. You may want to spend some time reflecting on Jesus' frustration at dealing with these disciples who appear to be such slow learners. Can you imagine Jesus' disappointment upon discovering that while he was speaking of his suffering and death, poor James and John were yearning to be successors to an earthly throne?

The prediction, misunderstanding and teaching pattern provides deeper insight into the message of Mark's Gospel. Through it, Mark teaches you what it *truly* means to be a disciple: a follower of Jesus, one who is sent, one who must take up the cross and follow Jesus (8:34), must lose his or her life for Jesus' sake (8:35), must be last and a servant (9:35) and must be a slave and servant to all (10:42-46).

Discipleship takes on a new meaning for the follower of Jesus in Mark's Gospel. The disciple is a member of Jesus' family when he or she follows the example given by Jesus, the example of servanthood and suffering. Pause for a few minutes and in the quiet of your heart dwell on this message of servanthood and discipleship.

Looking Back

On Journey 7 you made the following discoveries:

- The Marcan "sandwich" combines disparate points into a complete unit of understanding.
- Kinship to Jesus is a matter of faith and not necessarily of blood ties.
- Mark presents a definite pattern of prediction, misunderstanding and teaching to reveal the disciples' misconceptions of Jesus.
- The call to discipleship is a call to servanthood and suffering.

For Further Exploration

Kelber, Werner. *Mark's Story of Jesus*. Philadelphia: Fortress Press, 1979.

LaVerdiere, Eugene. *The Gospel of Mark: An Adventure in Scripture Study*, Videocassettes, 4 Series. Chicago: Dominican Central Productions, 1986.

Journey 8

Blindness and Discipleship

Journey 7 presented a scenario of prediction, misunderstanding and teaching via the disciples. They were presented as people who did not fully understand Jesus' role. You already have witnessed Peter's misunderstanding in his attempt to rebuke Jesus (8:32b), the disciples' concern for greatness (9:34) and the foolishness of James and John (10:35). Jesus' comments to the disciples (9:35) and James and John (10:42-46) are clear; further explanation, however, is needed regarding Jesus' comment to Peter.

Previous to Peter's misunderstanding, he had made his great profession: "You are the Messiah!" (8:29). Now Jesus has harsh words for Peter: "Get out of my sight, you satan!" (8:33). At first glance you may wonder why Jesus is so upset. After all, Peter merely is requesting Jesus not to go to Jerusalem where he is predicting suffering and death. Peter's words are an obvious plea from one friend to another who is facing destruction.

Mark's intention, however, is different. He does not give us a picture of Peter as a concerned friend but rather as a person who misunderstands the mission of Jesus. The Messiah, correctly professed by Peter in 8:29, is a messiah who is going to suffer and die. Jesus rebukes Peter because he is asking Jesus to be a different type of messiah and is *tempting* Jesus (like Satan in 1:12) not to continue with his mission.

Mark also presents the mission of Jesus and the misunderstanding of the disciples through two stories of blindness. In this exercise you will reflect on these two stories.

Discovering

Read Mark 8:22-26.

In the story of the blind man at Bethsaida, the following occurs:

- People bring a blind man to Jesus and ask Jesus to touch him.
- Jesus takes the man and puts spittle on his eyes.
- The man claims his vision is blurry ("I can see people but they look like walking trees!" [8:24]).
- Jesus lays hands on the man again and he sees everything clearly.

Reflecting on this story as a prologue to the triple account of prediction, misunderstanding and teaching, what connections can you make between the blind man at

Bethsaida and the misunderstanding of the disciples?

Summarize your connections between these two stories: the blind man and the misunderstanding of the disciples.

Exploring

Is it possible that Mark is comparing the blind man at Bethsaida to the disciples? Perhaps Mark is saying that the disciples' faith is blurred and cloudy. When will they truly see? For Mark, the disciples will see when they comprehend Jesus' teachings of servanthood and suffering. They will truly understand when they realize the full impact of the cross.

Notice the subtle movement in Mark's Gospel. The blind man of Bethsaida moves from *blindness* (lack of sight) to *sight* (although blurry) to *insight* (seeing things clearly). The disciples also are moving in their understanding of Jesus: blindness to sight to insight.

Discovering

Now read the second story of blindness, Mark 10:46-52.

Exploring

In this story of Bartimaeus, the following occurs:

- A blind beggar calls out, "Jesus, Son of David, have pity on me!"

- People tell the blind beggar to be quiet, but he screams all the louder.
- Jesus calls the man to him.
- Bartimaeus throws off his cloak and jumps up, moving towards Jesus.
- After being asked what he wants, the blind man asks for sight ("I want to see" [10:51].).
- Jesus tells him his faith has healed him.
- The man receives his sight.
- The man follows Jesus "up the road" (10:52).

Notice the action of the blind Bartimaeus: He screams for help; he wants to see. He throws off his cloak, he jumps up when called and he follows up the road. But where is Bartimaeus going with Jesus? The answer is in 11:1: "Then, as they neared Bethphage and Bethany on the Mount of Olives, close to Jerusalem...." Bartimaeus is going to Jerusalem. Obviously, what is going to happen in Jerusalem is Jesus' suffering and death. Jerusalem becomes the place where one receives insight into who Jesus really is.

The actions of these stories are parallel. Like the blind man at Bethsaida, Bartimaeus moves from blindness to sight to insight. His insight is faith in Jesus. It is this faith that encourages Bartimaeus to follow Jesus on the road to suffering and servanthood—a road that Mark has presented in the three teaching accounts occurring between the two blind men's stories.

Reflection on these two stories of blindness and the pattern of prediction, misunderstanding and teaching provides a rich insight to Mark's Gospel. If you incorporate the mimetic device and want to be a disciple of Christ, you, too, must take the path from blindness to sight to insight. The insight you receive is the same as that of Bartimaeus and the disciples: You must follow Jesus on the road of servanthood and suffering.

The study of these accounts also provides a clear understanding of Mark's healing stories. Each story has various layers of clarity which allow you to move from the literal meaning to the deeper theological meaning. As you move from one layer to the other, your understanding deepens.

- The *first level* is the literal words of the two healing stories of blind men. Simply, Jesus heals two men.
- The *second level* is Mark's address to his own community. Perhaps they are people in need of insight in the matter of servanthood and suffering. Remember, during Mark's time Christians suffer and are persecuted. Mark may be asking his community to reflect on the suffering of Jesus and how this suffering is a true sign of discipleship.
- In the *third level* Mark is asking you (the reader) if you

understand what it means to be a disciple. If you have been following the story, then you, too, realize that you are called to servanthood and suffering.

Often when I teach this section in parish communities, I am confronted with the question: Is Mark referring to literal suffering here? My response is "Yes!" In Mark's time literal suffering was occurring within the community.

This response prompts the question: How can we go through this literal suffering since none of us will ever be asked to die for the faith? My response to the second question is not always as quick. I agree that few of us will be asked to die for the faith. But, perhaps, we can still apply this question to our own times.

The question allows us to reflect on how we are the *cause* of suffering rather than on facing actual death like Mark's community. I am responsible for the suffering of the world by my *nonreflective* attitude toward it. My emphasis on *nonreflective* is deliberate. I believe that I, too, often fail to reflect on my lack of concern for humanity. Often my actions reveal an inadequate attempt to serve the alienated of my community. I am often silent when faced with injustice and too caught in a "consumerism" which leads to greed.

There is an additional reflection from this question. Today suffering is evident in the lives of many: the families who struggle daily with divorce, poverty, homelessness, disruption and chaos; those who continue to be the brunt of prejudices; men and women who suffer from stress, anxiety and fears. Mark calls us to reflect on our personal suffering, the sufferings of the world, and, more importantly, our desire to change our lives when they contribute to the suffering of others.

Looking Back

On Journey 8 you made the following discoveries:

- Peter's profession in 8:29 is correct, but it needs clarification. Jesus is the Messiah who will suffer and die. This is the point that Peter misunderstands.
- The story of the blind man at Bethsaida becomes a symbol of the disciples' understanding of Jesus.
- The story of Bartimaeus reinforces the notion that true discipleship is found in Jerusalem at the cross.
- All of us must move from blindness to sight to insight.

For Further Exploration

Harrington, Wilfred. *Mark*. New Testament Message, Vol. 4. Wilmington, Del.: Michael Glazier, Inc., 1979.

Journey 9

Reflections on Your Journey

Journey 3 introduced reflective exercises. Here in Journey 9 you again reflect on Mark's images of Jesus in order to discover the true meaning of your own journey. These reflective exercises provide an opportunity to speak to Jesus in an open and trusting fashion, to express your personal doubts, fears and joys.

Within this Journey, you will incorporate what you learned from previous exercises. A healing story will introduce you to a reflective technique that applies to all the miracle stories in the Gospel.

Read through the entire exercise in order to become comfortable with the steps proposed. Then, after the initial reading, do the reflective exercise.

Discovery

- Find a place that is relatively quiet. You will need at least 40 minutes to perform this exercise.
- Sit in a chair with your feet flat on the floor, your hands in your lap, your back straight, your eyes lowered or closed.
- Place your Bible on your lap and open it to Mark 10:46-52. (I have selected Bartimaeus' story because it is familiar from the previous Journey.) Also, keep a pencil or pen nearby.
- Relax your body by concentrating on your breathing. In the beginning moments of inhaling and exhaling, imagine the following: (1) inhale light, peace, relaxation; (2) exhale fear, anxiety, darkness. Attempt to establish a slow, steady rhythm of inhaling and exhaling.
- Read the biblical passage slowly.
- After reading the story of Bartimaeus, imagine yourself as an onlooker at this biblical scene. Place yourself in the scene by stationing yourself near a tree, a well or within the crowd.
- Use as many of your senses as possible. Hear the voices of people, look at their clothing and features, touch their garments, smell the air and so on.
- Notice the blind man sitting by the road. Spend some time studying this man.
- Hear the excitement of the crowd as Jesus approaches. Spend some time looking at Jesus.
- Hear the shouts of the blind man asking Jesus to heal him. Notice all of the activity: the crowd instructing Bartimaeus to be silent, Jesus halting.
- See Bartimaeus jump up when called by Jesus. Notice how quickly he throws off his cloak.

- Feel the excitement of Bartimaeus when his sight is restored. Spend some time contemplating this scene. Try to enter into Bartimaeus' celebration.
- Remove all other characters from the scene until there are only Jesus, Bartimaeus and you.
- Remove Bartimaeus from the scene so that there is only Jesus and you.
- In the manner most comfortable to you, speak to Jesus.
- When your conversation has concluded, say goodbye to Jesus in a manner that is comfortable for you.
- When you are ready, open your eyes, take a pencil or pen, write any ideas that come to you. Feel free to express your feelings in prose, poetry or drawings. Use the space provided for your written reflection.

Throughout your study of Mark, you might use this technique for any of the passages found in the Gospel. You need not limit yourself to healing stories only. You can place yourself at the Transfiguration (9:2-8), the Agony in the Garden (14:32-42) or the Crucifixion (15:23-39).

Looking Back

On Journey 9 you made the following discoveries:

Journey 10
Son of God/Son of Man

During my childhood, our sandlot football squad hoped desperately each season for a bigger and stronger kid to move into the neighborhood, someone to star on the team. Only in one August in all the Augusts of waiting did any new kid—a boy named John—show up on the block. Rumor had it that John was going to be our salvation. But when moving vans and automobiles finally produced John, he was discovered to be two years younger and 20 pounds lighter than any of our motley crew. So we faced another season of playing mediocre football, a season in which we weren't the worst, we certainly were not the best—we just *were*.

The background to the "Son of Man" and "Son of God" titles for Jesus in Mark's Gospel is similar to the ploys of my athletic career. Just as my team was waiting for a new person to offer us salvation, first-century Jews groaning under Roman oppression were waiting for a "new kid on the block." They looked for someone who would rid them of their helplessness and become a strong military and political leader: the Messiah. You can imagine their surprise and disappointment when the new person who enters the scene is Jesus: "Is this not the carpenter, the son of Mary, a brother of James and Joses and Judas and Simon?" (6:3). Not only is there difficulty with Jesus' background, but there is further difficulty with his "political platform."

When Mark wrote his Gospel around A.D. 70, the situation was still chaotic. Christians were waiting for the return of a "special" Jesus to bring salvation. Mark, through his Gospel, is instructing his community that their great hope of salvation is quite different from what they expect.

Discovering

Read and reflect on the following passages: Mark 10:15; 10:29-31; 12:31b-34; and 12:42-44.

Exploring

In those passages you read reminders that Jesus' advice is to be childlike, to be willing to die, to be a servant and to be able to give oneself totally. Certainly this is not the message of a strong military leader.

What is worse is Mark's picture of the people with whom Jesus associates.

Discovering

Read and reflect on the following passages: Mark 1:40-41; 2:23-24; and 7:24-30.

Exploring

Now the expected leader, who is not the great warrior-hero, turns out to be a man who associates with the alienated (lepers and a Gentile woman) and breaks the sabbath law! (At this time, a Jew did not associate with a Gentile [non-Jew] and men never associated with women in public. Notice the countercultural Jesus in 7:24-30.)

If Jesus is not to be the expected leader, then he must be something else. For Mark, Jesus is certainly the Christ (the Anointed One), but only on his Father's terms. This presentation of Jesus in his Father's terms is expressed for Mark in the titles: "Son of God" and "Son of Man." These titles are rooted in the Hebrew Scriptures (Old Testament). On this Journey you will investigate the background of these titles in reading the Book of Isaiah and the Book of Daniel.

Discovering

Read Isaiah 52:13—53:12. (The Book of Isaiah is found in the Hebrew Scriptures, the Old Testament, between the Books of Sirach and Jeremiah.)

Summarize in a phrase or sentence the leadership qualities of Jesus that are presented in Isaiah.

Exploring

With this background from Isaiah, refresh your memory of the Son of God statements found in the following passages: Mark 1:1; 1:11; 3:11; 14:61-62a; and 15:39.

Your previous work with some of these passages (see especially Journeys 2 and 6) helped you recognize that the title "Son of God" is proclaimed by believers in 1:1 and by the Father in 1:11. It is a mystery realized by the demons (3:11) and admitted by Jesus (14:62a). Even the centurion (15:39) makes this proclamation—but only after the crucifixion. You saw in Journey 2 that this title has nothing to do with biological sonship.

Mark did not invent the title *Son of God*. Known throughout the Hellenistic (Greek) world, it referred to a divine person who was filled with wisdom and able to perform miracles. In our modern-day perception, the "Son of God" would be a superman-type figure. What Mark does differently from the Hellenistic thought is to elaborate on the title *Son of God*. This elaboration is clarified by the title *Son of Man*—a title you will explore later in this Journey.

The title *Son of God*, understood against a background of the Isaiah passages, relates to a suffering servant, not to a miracle worker. Mark is intent on our understanding this point. Mark does not want us to confuse Jesus with a miracle-worker but to understand the true meaning of Jesus.

Discovering

Read the following passages: Mark 1:25; 1:34; 1:43-44; 3:12; 5:43; 7:36; 8:26; 8:30; and 9:9.

Exploring

The message in these nine passages is clear. The one healed or witnessing God's manifestation in Jesus is instructed to be silent. The point is obvious and can be paraphrased in the following way: "Do not say anything about this event lest you misunderstand." This is not a miracle-worker or a divine person in a Hellenistic sense but the Son of God whom you will fully understand only *after he has gone through his suffering*. This is why there is no secret for the centurion (15:39). He is the only *human* in the Gospel to proclaim Jesus as the Son of God, and he makes his profession at the foot of the cross.

The perception of Jesus as the God-man or Son of God is crucial. Many times in biblical studies, you will read or hear various interpretations regarding the miracles of Jesus. Occasionally, you may be instructed that these miracles did not occur as written in the text. The point is not to deny the miracles but to force you to investigate where your faith truly lies. Do you believe in a miracle-worker only, or do you believe in a Jesus who suffered, died and rose from the dead? If your faith is rooted in the latter, you can then understand the full meaning of the miracle stories.

Discovering

Now read the following passages about the "Son of Man": Mark 2:10; 9:9; 9:12; 9:31; 10:33-34; 10:45; 14:21; and 14:41.

Summarize your understanding of the above passages.

Again, remembering the background from Isaiah, you can associate the Isaiah passages with the above Marcan passages on the "Son of Man." Jesus is the "Son of Man" who is a *suffering servant who is going to be handed over to enemies and killed*.

Discovering

Mark presents another image of Jesus as "Son of Man" which complements the Isaiah theme. This image comes from the Book of Daniel (found in the Hebrew Scriptures between Ezekiel and Hosea). Daniel 7 contains a great deal of dream imagery and symbolic language.

To help you with Daniel 7, remember that this dream sequence refers to a future judgment scene. Often biblical scholars refer to this scene as *eschatological* (concerning itself with the last things). Daniel presents an eschatological judgment scene in which the Son of Man will come as the final judge of creation. Mark will incorporate this imagery in the passages you will be asked to read and summarize next.

Read Daniel 7 to familiarize yourself with some of the ideas presented.

Read and summarize Mark 8:38; 13:26; 14:62.

Exploring

This image of the "Son of Man" is exactly what you read in Daniel 7. The "Son of Man" will come in glory with the clouds of heaven.

The two images bound together (Son of God and Son of Man) present a complete portrait of Jesus. Jesus is the one presented by the Father. He is presented on the Father's terms and not ours. He is not a mere miracle-worker or warrior hero. Rather, Jesus is the suffering servant who has given his life for his friends; because of this event he will judge the entire world. The two titles (*Son of God* and *Son of Man*) complement each other and give the fullest understanding of this Christ.

During the time of Mark, the title *Son of Man* was understood by some people as a title of majesty. But Mark uses the title with a more profound significance than mere majesty. For Mark, Jesus is the "Son of Man," an elaboration of the "Son of God." Because Jesus is willing to be the suffering servant, he takes on a position of majesty as ruler and judge of all creation.

Looking Back

On Journey 10 you made the following discoveries:

- The titles *Son of God* and *Son of Man* are complementary to each other and give the full picture of who Jesus is.
- "Son of God" is taken from the Hebrew Scriptures (Old Testament). It had some appeal to the Hellenistic world which also used the term. Mark uses the title not to express a mere miracle-worker but for one who is a servant and is willing to suffer. The background for this title rests in Isaiah 52.
- "Son of Man," from Daniel 7, is attributed to Jesus because of his willingness to be the suffering servant as evidenced through his death and resurrection. Jesus, the Son of Man, will rule and judge the world.
- The complementary elements of these titles are not understood until one sees the cross. Here the believer proclaims with the centurion, "Clearly this man was the Son of God" (15:39).

For Further Exploration

Fuller, Reginald and Pheme Perkins. *Who Is This Christ?* Philadelphia: Fortress Press, 1984.

Kee, Howard Clark. *Community of a New Age: Studies in Mark's Gospel.* Philadelphia: Westminster Press, 1977.

Kingsbury, Jack Dean. *The Christology of Mark's Gospel.* Philadelphia: Fortress Press, 1983.

Journey 11

Loaves, Water and the Transfiguration

With an understanding of the two major titles for Jesus, you are able now to investigate some prominent stories in Mark's Gospel. In this exercise you will concentrate on two feeding stories (chapters 6 and 8), the walking on water story (6:45 ff.) and the Transfiguration (9:2-9).

Discovering

Mark presents two feeding stories in his Gospel. You will read the two accounts in which you will find the feeding stories and additional information.

Read Mark 6:34-7:37 and 8:1-26.

In the space provided jot down the broad sequence of events that are given in these two accounts. Limit your listings to *similarities* between the two stories rather than differences.

Mark 6

Mark 8

Exploring

Next you will find listed some parallels between the two stories. Do not be concerned if they are not exactly the same as yours. The purpose is to have a listing for discussion. The parallels I am listing are taken from *Mark, Matthew, Luke: A Guide to the Gospel Parallels*, by Neil Flanagan, O.S.M.

6:30-34 Feeding of 5000	8:1-9 Feeding of 4000
6:45-52 Crossing to Bethsaida	8:10 Crossing to Dalmanuth
6:52 Loaves not understood	8:14-21 Loaves not understood
7:1-23 Against Pharisees	8:11-13 Against Pharisees
7:31-37 Healing deaf man	8:23-26 Healing blind man

The similarities between these two accounts prompt a variety of opinions by biblical scholars. Some believe there were two distinct feeding events, while others view the event as two versions of one feeding. We do know that Mark believes the accounts to be so important that he tells either both stories or both versions of the same story. You are free to choose any one of these opinions. Whatever your opinion regarding the origin of the two stories, the following exercise will help you to discover their importance.

Discovering

Skim through the two accounts and find the following information:

How many loaves remained after feeding 5000?

How many loaves remained after feeding 4000?

Exploring

Numerology (the significance of numbers and their meanings) played an important part in biblical writing. The number of baskets remaining provides clues to biblical scholars.

After the feeding of 5000, 12 baskets remained; the feeding of 4000 produced seven remaining baskets. The *12* baskets represent the *12* tribes of Israel mentioned in the Hebrew Scriptures. Mark 6 is a Jewish version of the story.

The number *seven* is a perfect number in the Hellenistic world. For the person of Mark's time, *seven* is a combination of the number three (representative of God) and the number four (representative of the world). Thus *seven* contains all things: God and the world. In the account with *seven* baskets remaining, you have a Gentile (non-Jewish) version of the feeding stories. Placing both numbers together (12 and seven), there is a story that is applicable to all peoples of the world, that is, Jew and Gentile.

Additional background study in the significance of these accounts helps you to reflect on the importance of the loaves. Here you must once more refer to the Hebrew Scriptures.

Discovering

Read Exodus 16.

Exploring

In this account from the Hebrew Scriptures, the Israelites are being fed "manna" from heaven while wandering in the desert. Notice in the Marcan accounts "This is a *deserted* place..." (6:35) and, in 8:4, "How can anyone give these people sufficient bread in this *deserted* spot?" (emphasis added).

Mark's two references to a *deserted* spot is more than a coincidence. He wants to recall the feeding in the desert when God took care of God's people. If you do not remember the story of feeding in the Hebrew Scripture, you will not fully understand these two feedings.

Discovering

Look again at the misunderstanding statements of 8:17-21.

Exploring

In this account Mark is spotlighting the disciples' misunderstanding. Notice in the account that Jesus asks: "Are your minds completely blinded? Have you eyes but no sight? Ears but no hearing?"

In the parallel listing (p. 33), notice that the two accounts conclude with stories of healings of a deaf man (7:31-37) and a blind man (8:23-26). The importance of these two healing stories is not the *physical* healing of blindness and deafness, but *spiritual* healing. It is in the spiritual healing that we receive the sight of faith and hear the words of faith and then understand the meaning of the loaves.

Mark's community understood the meaning of the loaves in their eucharistic bread. The true understanding of the loaves comes in the spiritual awareness of the meaning of Eucharist. This eucharistic bread of the Marcan community was received by both Jews and Gentiles who accepted the eucharistic Jesus as Messiah, Son of Man and Son of God.

Discovering

At first glance, the story of walking on water appears to have little connection with the feeding stories. Yet the close sequence of feeding and water is found in the writings of Matthew (Matthew 14) as well as Mark. Just as the feeding stories are rooted in the Hebrew Scriptures, so an understanding of water is found in the Hebrew Scriptures.

Read the following accounts and trace the image of

water presented in these accounts: Genesis 1:6 and 7:6-10; Exodus 14:23-31; and Mark 4:35-41.

In the space provided write one or two sentences about your understanding of water in these accounts.

Exploring

In the creation story (Genesis 1:6) water needs to be contained to stop its chaotic activity. What was a formless wasteland is now an ordered creation of earth and water set by God.

In the account of Noah and his family (Genesis 7:6-10) water is destructive. Only Noah and the passengers of his ark float atop the chaotic waters of death.

In Exodus 14:23-31 the Israelites are faced with death from two sides: the Egyptians who are pursuing them and the waters of the Red Sea. It is God who separates the water, allowing them to pass through on dry land. Then the water returns as destructive activity and kills the evil Egyptians.

Finally, water is chaotic in Mark 4. Here, water is frightening: The disciples believe they will drown. Jesus calms the water and questions the disciples' faith.

In all of these accounts water is seen as a destructive element. Although each of these accounts presents water as literal destruction, there is a difference in the symbolic significance of water. In some stories from the Hebrew Scriptures water symbolizes death or sin, while in the Christian Scriptures water symbolizes death or lack of faith.

Against this background of water as a destructive element, Mark has Jesus walking on water. Taken symbolically, the waters of death are no match for the one who is to overcome death. Jesus, who is truth and grace, will conquer death on the cross. What was once out of control and a sign of death is now so peaceful and calm that the Messiah is able to walk on it.

Certainly for the Marcan community and for all people of faith, water has a connection to Baptism. In Baptism one is plunged into the depths of the water as a sign of death to sin, only to come out to new life and salvation. The two symbols—water and loaves, Baptism and Eucharist—are the central expressions of the Christian faith. Baptism gives eyes and ears to the faith that is expressed in the Eucharist.

Finally, the person who understands the Hebrew Scriptures connects the great event of the Israelites escaping through the separated Sea and being fed manna in the desert with the feeding by Jesus and his walking on water. This is the reason why the two stories are placed so closely together in both Mark and Matthew's Gospels.

To recapitulate, you began studying two accounts of feeding stories within the Gospel. In the beginning you listed the literal connections between these stories. The next step viewed background information to the stories from either the Hebrew Scriptures or from the culture of Mark's time. You then probed the symbolic details of the stories, recognizing the importance of numbers and the understanding of water as death. You were able to connect the symbolic understandings of loaves and water in the Hebrew Scriptures with the Marcan community. Finally, you were able to connect an understanding of loaves and water to the faith understanding of Eucharist and Baptism.

This study of the two feeding stories prepares you to observe biblical accounts in two fashions: the literal accounts and, more importantly, their symbolic significance to your faith journey. The question of two distinct feeding stories versus one feeding story with two versions is insignificant when the feeding stories are seen in relation to the sacraments of Baptism and Eucharist. May all people of faith always have eyes to see and ears to hear the Word of God!

Discovering

The study of the Transfiguration story clarifies two points: the title Son of God, which was discussed in Journey 10, and why the disciples continue to misunderstand.

To place this account in its proper perspective, reflect again on Mark 8:29, a key point in Mark's structure. Remember that the first half of Mark's Gospel climaxes with Peter's great profession of faith, "You are the Messiah!" With Peter's words ringing in your ears, now read Mark 9:2-13.

First, notice that Jesus has taken an inner circle of friends to a high mountain. You may be reminded of another significant mountain, Sinai (see Exodus 19:16-25). In the Exodus account, God appears to Moses with trumpet blasts, fire and smoke. God speaks in thunder. This appearance of God in nature (thunder, fire, smoke) is referred to as a *theophany*. Therefore, the signal words "high mountain" prepare you for another theophany: one that clarifies Peter's proclamation.

Now find the theophany in Mark's account of the Transfiguration.

Exploring

In my Bible, Mark 9:7 reads: "This is my Son, my beloved. Listen to him." These words from God are similar to the words revealed to Jesus and us in the baptismal story (Mark 1:11). The difference here is that the revelation is also *to the three disciples.*

The disciples, however, still do not understand. Even though they *see* the transformed Christ and *hear* the words of God, they fail to comprehend the message. Their lack of understanding is revealed in the reason Peter was nearly at a loss for words: "for they were all overcome with awe" (9:6). (Other translations say that they were "overcome with fear," "so terrified." Fear [or awe] is understood as the opposite of faith and understanding.)

Even though Peter has made his great proclamation in 8:29 he continues to misunderstand. Peter's statement in itself is correct; he recognizes the Messiah, however, only after witnessing healings and exorcisms. He still does not understand the full implications of Jesus' Messiahship. Total understanding will be obtained at the cross or after the Resurrection.

For now, Mark writes: "They kept this word of his to themselves, though they continued to discuss what 'to rise from the dead' meant" (9:10). We can assume that the disciples understood the answer to their questions after the Resurrection, since the Book of Acts records that Peter and the disciples preached the true meaning of Messiah (Acts 2). At the Transfiguration, it was meaningless for them to want to erect three booths (monuments) since the passion, death and resurrection of Jesus had not yet taken place.

During the Transfiguration, notice that Christ's clothes become "white—whiter than the work of any bleacher could make them" (9:3). The image of Jesus transfigured is similar to accounts in the Book of Daniel.

Discovering

Read Daniel 7:9 and 12:3.

Exploring

These two verses from the Book of Daniel portray an eschatological figure who is to come at the endtime with clothes whiter than white. (Remember, *eschatological* refers to the "last things.") Jesus will become this figure after the Resurrection. Thus, the Transfiguration account is an anticipation of Jesus' Resurrection glory.

The other two characters in this story of the Transfiguration are Elijah and Moses. In the Hebrew Scriptures there is no greater person than Moses. Careful reading of Mark 9:2-13 shows that Moses as well as Elijah disappear when the great theophany is given: "This is my Son, my beloved..." (9:7). The central character is Jesus, who will *perfect* the Hebrew Scriptures' revelation: the Law (Moses) and the prophets (Elijah).

Mark emphasizes Elijah in the Transfiguration and in the events that immediately follow (9:9-13). The Jewish tradition firmly held that Elijah would appear before the Messiah came. This tradition is based on Malachi 3:2-3. Elijah is to come to prepare the people for the Messiah, who will then judge the world. To this day, Jewish families place the Elijah cup at their Passover meal as a reminder that they wait for Elijah, who will announce the coming of the Messiah.

Elijah's preparation is inspiring repentance. In Mark 9:11 the disciples imply that Elijah has not come. Jesus responds that Elijah *has* come in John the Baptist (9:12). John, the Elijah figure, has announced the need for repentance (1:4). Moreover, John is the true Elijah figure since he has already proved himself as a suffering servant. He has prepared the way for the Messiah even to the point of imitating the Messiah by going to his own death at the scheming of Herodias (6:27).

Looking Back

On Journey 11 you made the following discoveries:

- The two feeding stories present a picture of the total world of Jew and Gentile.
- Numerology (the significance of numbers and their meanings) is important to biblical study.
- Although the literal presentation of the stories is important, a much deeper understanding is found in the symbolic meaning of the accounts. Further insight is gained when the Hebrew Scriptures are used as background information.
- The two feeding stories display the importance of Baptism and Eucharist for the Marcan community and all communities of believers.
- The transfiguration is misunderstood by the disciples until they fully understand the cross.
- The Elijah figure has come in the person of John the Baptist.

For Further Exploration

Anderson, Bernhard. *Understanding the Old Testament.* Englewood Cliffs, N.J.: Prentice Hall, 1984.

LaVerdiere, Eugene. *The Gospel of Mark: An Adventure in Scripture Study*, Videocassettes, 4 Series. Chicago: Dominican Central Productions, 1986.

Journey 12

Hidden Message

Arthur Miller wrote *The Crucible* in the 1950's. The play captures the intrigue of witch-hunting in Salem, Massachusetts, in the 1600's. Miller dramatizes this terrible glimpse of American history through characters so caught up in fanaticism that they are willing to sacrifice other members of their community.

The audience witnesses the interaction between the characters and events without having to know anything about Salem in the 1600's or about Miller. But when viewers understand Miller's time and work, they see that Miller is also portraying the 1950's, a time when McCarthyism made many artists the object of "witch-hunts," made them enemies of the American government. Miller demonstrates the absurdity of the events of his own time by presenting the bizarre behavior of another time.

There is a connection to be drawn between Miller's writing style and the use of biblical material. For a period of 400 years (200 B.C. to A.D. 200), one popular literary form in biblical times was referred to as *apocalyptic*. This style contained hidden messages relayed in highly symbolic language. Just as playwright Miller compared one historical time with another, the biblical writer in his apocalyptic style draws on current situations but inserts them in past times.

Apocalyptic techniques became popular during times of extreme chaos and persecution. Evidence of the style is discovered in the Book of Daniel and the Book of Revelation. Each text reflects a period filled with extreme hardship at the hands of horrible tyrants who ordered unspeakable atrocities against many people. The apocalyptic writer offers hope to his readers in a time of great confusion. Although the language is highly symbolic, it is understood by the individual who is aware of its symbolic meanings.

In addition to the Book of Daniel and the Book of Revelation, apocalyptic material influenced much of the Gospel material. Mark adapts this literary style within his Gospel, especially in Chapter 13.

Discovering

Read Mark 13.

Exegesis is a line-by-line explanation of a biblical text. This biblical tool allows the student to become acquainted with the symbolic meaning of the language, literary styles of the writers and customs of the time. The exercise which follows will provide an introduction to exegesis of a text.

In the following exercise, reread Mark 13 according to the prescribed sections. After reading the verses, write a short summary of the message given or the image portrayed.

Mark 13:1-2

Mark 13:3-4

Mark 13:5-6

Mark 13:7-8

Mark 13:9-13

Mark 13:14-20

Mark 13:32

Mark 13:21-23

Mark 13:33-36

Mark 13:24-27

Mark 13:37

Mark 13:28-29

Mark 13:30

Mark 13:31

Discovering

In this exercise you will investigate each summary. Compare your writings with the suggestions presented here.

Scene One (13:1-2): Jesus forecasts the destruction of the Temple to one of his disciples.

Read Mark 11:11-25.

This reading from Chapter 11 demonstrates Mark's preoccupation with the Temple, one of the remarkable buildings of its time. Despite its towering structure, Jesus predicts its total destruction. Just as the fig tree (11:12-14; 20-21) is destroyed, so too the Temple will be destroyed (13:1-2).

In the apocalyptic style the writer often places a past event as a future happening, thus allowing the writer to deal with the future repercussions of the event. In other words, some scholars believe that by the time of Mark's writing the destruction of the Temple was an accomplished fact. The Temple was destroyed with the fall of Jerusalem to Titus during the Jewish wars of A.D. 66-70.

Because Mark strongly suggests the Temple destruction as the background to this chapter, scholars date Mark's writing within this period, thus the common dating of Mark's Gospel at A.D. 70. Since the Christians of the time were attuned to apocalyptic material, they believed the destruction of the Temple to be the last event before Jesus' final return in glory. But when the Temple was destroyed and Jesus did not come, Mark had to deal with the discouragement within his community.

Scene Two (13:3-4): Further instruction on the Temple destruction.

Additional hidden messages are presented in these two verses. The Mount of Olives, although a real place, held a symbolic association with the coming of the Messiah. The prophet Zechariah writes, "That day his feet shall rest upon the Mount of Olives, which is opposite Jerusalem to the east. The Mount of Olives shall be cleft in two from east to west by a very deep valley, and half of the mountain shall move to the north and half of it to the south" (Zechariah 14:4).

Jesus, the one who was promised and who will come again at the endtime, is seated upon the mountain gazing down on the doomed city of Jerusalem. Although Jesus is directing his comments to four disciples, we can assume that Mark is responding to difficulties within his community. There are two questions here: When will the Temple be destroyed (referring to 13:2)? What sign will precede the final end?

Remember, there was a close linkage between the destruction of the Temple and Jesus' second coming (*parousia*) in the minds of Mark's community. The disciples, symbolizing Mark's community, are confused since the Temple has been destroyed yet the *parousia* has not occurred.

In our own time we are confronted by individuals who claim to read the "signs of the times" and predict the world's end. Comparing the statehood of Israel or the nuclear armament of the world powers with biblical imagery, these endtime predictors wait anxiously for the world's destruction. Their constant hope is that they will be "raptured"—lifted bodily into heaven—just before the final holocaust which will destroy the planet. The biblical foundation for this belief is obtained from an archaic translation of 1 Thessalonians 4:17.

Scene Three (13:5-23): Signs and warnings.

This scene contains five messages.

1) Mark 13:5-6 warns against false prophets. The scene opens and concludes with the same command to be on one's guard (13:5, 23) against false prophets who claim either to be the Christ or to know exactly when and where the Christ will appear. Just as Jesus warns the disciples against false prophets in these scenes, Mark is warning his community of false prophets within their ranks. The tense atmosphere of Mark's time produced numerous

fanatics who announced either that they were Jesus or that the end of the world was coming. This must have been a common problem in the early Church, since other scriptural accounts warn against the same happenings (2 Thessalonians 2; Acts 20:29-30).

The problem of false prophets continues to this day. While living in New York City I saw vast numbers of endtime predictors positioned on Manhattan streetcorners, screaming at theatergoers about their sin and their need for repentance because the end was at hand. Some radio and television programs also abound with fanatic predictions of doomsday close at hand.

2) Mark 13:7-8 speaks of wars and rumors of war. Mark, through Jesus, informs us "this is not yet the end" (13:7). Although the apocalyptic writing is filled with disasters (wars, earthquakes and famine) as signs of the endtime, the actual endtime has not occurred. Mark merely states "Such things are bound to happen" (13:7). For Mark, this is not the "end" but rather the "beginning" of suffering for Christians (remember the title of the Gospel in 1:1). This beginning of suffering is developed in the remainder of the scene.

3) Mark 13:9-13 promises persecution and suffering. If you are a follower of Jesus, you will share his experience of suffering and persecution, a point you discovered in the mimetic device of Journey 5. For Mark, the death of a believer is not the *end* but the *beginning*. It is through death that the Good News will be proclaimed to all the Gentiles. Persecution and death was viewed by an early Christian from two points: The death itself bore witness to the belief in Jesus as Lord, which could encourage others into believing, and death is a beginning of a new life with Christ.

Another possible interpretation of these verses does not exclude the above. In Mark's time the chaos of the Jewish wars caused division and hatred among a number of parties. Even within parties, there were opposing camps. It is possible that this division and chaos also eroded families and relationships. Perhaps within the Marcan community members were hated by their families because of their love for Jesus. Again, Mark reminds the Christians that they are called to suffering, which is the true witness of a Christian life.

4) Mark 13:14 refers to "the abominable and destructive presence." This term comes directly from the Book of Daniel (Daniel 9:27; 11:31; 12:11), where it referred to a heathen altar built by Antiochus in 168 B.C. over the Temple altar. In choosing the reference Mark claims the present age is worse than the time of Antiochus; therefore, Christians are to be on guard. They are to guard against the "prince of the world" (Satan or evil) who now assumes his position on the spot which held the Temple. The

apocalyptic view realizes that the present world is under the power of Satan but will be transformed under the power of God when the Messiah comes again in glory.

The following verses (13:15-20) describe the action people take when their city is under threat of siege. With the enemies at the gate, the person must get out fast. The apocalyptic material, however, suggests a deeper meaning than the practicalities of avoiding the enemy. For Mark, the Christian flees the city under the throne of Satan and carries the message of salvation to those willing to believe in Jesus the Suffering Servant.

5) In Mark 13:21-23 we read again the repeated message to "be constantly on guard!" This time Mark warns that chaotic situations can recur. Throughout life, Christians will face many false prophets who will try to persuade them to abandon the faith. Mark indicates that all of Jesus' messages have "told you about it beforehand" (13:23). This statement on Jesus' lips signals that Jesus is the true prophet who is able to discern the true signs of the time. He is the true prophet since he has mentioned these things beforehand. Just as all previous predictions were true, this forewarning is true.

Scene Four (Mark 13:24-27): The Parousia.

The scene draws again on the Hebrew Scriptures. The Son of Man (Journey 10) will appear after these events. His true image will be manifested at the *parousia.* Then the Christian will truly *see* and *gain insight* into the mission of the Son of Man. For the Christian, this will be a time of rejoicing as the Son of Man gathers together all the people of God.

Scene Five (Mark 13:28-37): Watchfulness.

Again Mark draws on the actual events. Since Palestine is filled with evergreens, the fig tree is one of the few trees that brings forth buds in the spring. Symbolically, Mark states that the end is near. Mark and his community may have believed that Jesus' Second Coming would occur within their lifetime. (Paul makes similar claims in 1 Thessalonians 4:14-16.) But the exact certainty of the endtime is known only by the Father. It is the Father who reveals the endtime to the Son at the appropriate time. Mark 13:32 is the answer likewise to modern false prophets who insist on predicting the exact time for the end of the world.

Obviously, Mark's personal understanding that Christ will return during his own lifetime was incorrect. If, however, we stress Mark's concept of the endtime during his generation, we receive new insight to this message by dividing Christian events into three main categories:

• The foreshadowing of the Messiah—the period beginning with creation and ending with the coming of Jesus.
• The historical coming of the Messiah—the period when Jesus was on earth, his ministry and mission. This period ends with the death and resurrection.
• The in-between time until the Messiah comes again. This begins with the coming of the Spirit and the apostolic endeavor to proclaim Christ to the entire world. It will end when the Son of Man comes in his glory. It includes Mark and ourselves.

Like Mark and his followers, we are waiting for the endtime. It is when Jesus comes in his glory that we will gain *insight* into what it means to be a follower. For Mark and all of us, this will be a great day of rejoicing since we believe that it is at this time that God will join all God's people together. Like the blind man at Bethsaida (8:22), we will move from *blindness* to *sight* to *insight.*

Exploring

To conclude the remarks about apocalyptic material, I have listed key elements of apocalyptic literature under six broad headings:

1) Authorship. Apocalyptic literature is presented as the writing of some ancient patriarch or prophet who has long been dead. The historical inspired author adopts a literary pseudonym. Although this is not the entire case in Mark (or in the Book of Revelation) since we do not have a literary pseudonym, we do have Mark placing the apocalyptic scene on the lips of Jesus after Jesus has died and the Temple has been destroyed. (The suggestion that Mark places the scene on the "lips of Jesus" is part of the understanding gained in Journey 4. Remember the movement from what Jesus actually said to what was written about what Jesus said.)

2) Concept of God. Apocalyptic material understands God as "the Ancient One of Days" or *Adonai* (Lord). God is utterly transcendent and communicates with human history only through the medium of heavenly messengers. God is so holy that we should never pronounce the name, Yahweh, which was revealed to Moses.

3) Concept of Revelation. When we speak of the concept of revelation, we attempt to grasp how God reveals (unveils) God's self in time and history. In the apocalyptic material revelation is considered new information about God's plan for the world. This plan is a secret made known only to the very holy ones. To maintain the elements of secrecy, symbolic images and numbers are revealed as clues to comprehending the plan of God. In this section of Mark Jesus is the holy one of God who has had the secret revealed to him. He is unveiling this message in symbolic language.

4) Time of God's Revelation. Apocalyptic material stresses that Adonai spoke or unveiled the secret plan in some archaic past when things were different. Since then the plan has been sealed in secrecy until the appropriate time when one can disclose the secret based on certain signs. These "signs" point to the fact that God's power is going to be victorious in a final cosmic conflict in which good will triumph over evil.

5) Hope for the Human Future. Apocalyptic material finds hope for humankind in the absolute cosmic (though hidden) power of Adonai, who can do anything. Hope also is found in the community which endures martyrdom rather than compromise their belief in either God or the Law. Even the present escalation of suffering is only an apparent and momentary triumph of evil. The Day of Judgment will come out of the heavens in the twinkling of an eye as a cosmic miracle worked by Adonai. We need not despair even in the very bitterness of our present sufferings and persecution at the hands of the enemy. Because this entire contemporary world order is under the spell of evil, Adonai will make a new heaven and a new earth.

6) Faith. Apocalyptic material invites the community to have faith that Adonai is powerful enough to do anything. In this sense it invites us to a trust in Adonai which transcends our experiences of human knowing. Most or all of us have never seen an angel shut a lion's mouth (Daniel 6:23) or a prophet float off to another town (Ezekiel 3:12-14). But why or how could we deny that it is possible in Adonai's ultimate power?

Finally, the apocalyptic person gazes into the far reaches of heaven and cries out in anguish over the loss of good in human history and prays, "But you, O Lord, how long?"

Looking Back

On Journey 12, you made these discoveries:

- Mark 13 is an example of apocalyptic material which was a common literary form of the time.
- Exegetical material provides a line-by-line explanation of a biblical text emphasizing language, customs and literary style.

- Mark, through the apocalyptic style, provides a message of hope to his community during times of chaos and persecution.
- The true Christian, although suffering now, will ultimately enjoy the *parousia* when the Son of Man comes in glory.
- Apocalyptic material contains six key elements.

For Further Exploration

Hanson, James. *If I'm A Christian, Why Be a Catholic?: The Biblical Roots of Catholic Faith*. Ramsey, N.J.: Paulist Press, 1984.

Jewett, Robert. *Jesus Against the Rapture: Seven Unexpected Prophecies*. Philadelphia: Westminster Press, 1979.

Journey 13
The Way of the Cross

This manual provides an opportunity to reflect prayerfully on the full impact of Mark's Gospel. Journey 3 and Journey 9 introduced two techniques for reflecting on the Gospel. The first section of this Journey provides an additional exercise entitled, "Reflective Reading for Meditation."

People read in a variety of ways. Depending on the intention, they glance through an article and skim the contents of a page or chapter, or diligently pour over material to fully comprehend the writer's message. Reflective reading for meditation incorporates techniques which encourage the reader to combine both intellectual capabilities and spiritual growth. Its purpose is to engulf the person in the message. The biblical image is to "eat the text"—to find the words so sweet to your taste that like food, they become a part of one's being. This is not merely reading the Passion narrative of Mark but seeking to become one with it.

The techniques for reflective reading are few and provide great flexibility:

- Find a place "somewhat" quiet where you will not be disturbed. The quotation marks around *somewhat* are deliberate. Each person has a personal sense of quietness. Many people find the outdoors conducive to reflective reading for meditation. Others have success with reflective reading techniques at airports, in a doctor's office or riding on subways. For the majority of us, a quiet place at home will serve the purpose. The choice of location is up to you and depends on your ability to block out distracting and disturbing noises.

- Once the location is established, enhance the setting by creating a reflective atmosphere. Depending on the location, you can enthrone the Bible, decorate with flowers, display seasonal reminders or light candles to remind you of the presence of God. In busier locations merely place the Bible on your lap.

- Select the passage for reflective reading. For this next exercise, you will read Mark 14—15. While slowly reading the passages *move your lips*. This action slows the reading process and allows for deeper concentration on the material.

- Do not be alarmed if you do not finish the entire reading designated for the exercise. You may stop at the first line or spend the entire time reflecting on a word, idea or image.

- The time spent in reading and reflection is up to the individual. The total time, however, must be divided into two or three parts. If you are experimenting with reflective reading alone, provide equal time for reading and reflective writing. For the novice, a period of 10 minutes for reading and 10 minutes for writing is sufficient. Small groups may include a third time period for sharing.

- After meditating on the passage, begin *writing*. Allow the pen or pencil to guide itself. Although this sounds strange, the purpose is not to "think" about the writing but rather to allow the writing to flow from one's heart. You may find your writing expressed in poetry, song or even sketches.

- When the exercise is performed by a group, sharing is voluntary. The participants are free to share the whole of their writing, to summarize the writing in broad terms or merely to pass on this part of the exercise. Individuals should never be pressured to share their writing since it is very personal, as well as holy and special.

Discovering

Read Mark 14—15. Use the space provided for your reflective writing.

Discovering

Now we will examine key passages in Mark's Passion narrative. The remainder of this exercise changes its focus from reflective reading to discussion of key elements within the narrative.

Read Mark 14:3-9. Summarize the event in one or two sentences.

Exploring

Two elements are important for review with this passage: the *action* of the woman and the *words* of Jesus.

1) Action. The woman, not named, comes and anoints Jesus with a costly ointment. There is a strong objection (presumably by the disciples) to the waste of this perfume, which is compared in price to an individual's yearly wage. The woman's motivation appears to be a pure act of love. The Scriptures say nothing else of the woman's intention other than "She has done what she could" (14:8). Once her action is completed, she is never heard of again, although she is to be remembered "throughout the world" whenever the Good News is proclaimed. This anointing is in the tradition of another anointing found within the Hebrew Scriptures.

Read 2 Kings 9:1-13.

The passage is linked with this passage from Mark. Elisha's prophet anointing Jehu as "king over Israel" corresponds to the woman's anointing of Jesus as the true King of Israel.

2) Words. The second key element is Jesus' reaction to this act of love. He criticizes those objecting to the anointing with a remark similar to his criticism of the disciples when they turned away the children (Mark 10:14). For Jesus, this is a significant moment, since he associates the anointing with this death: "By perfuming my body she is anticipating its preparation for burial" (Mark 14:8b).

Jesus accepts the anointing appropriate for a king but relates it to a king who will suffer and die. Mark never fails to emphasize the suffering servant theme in his Gospel. Just as Peter did not realize the impact of his statement in

8:29, the woman does not realize the impact of her actions. Jesus explains again that he is the Messiah-King professed by Peter's words and the woman's actions, but a Messiah-King who also is Suffering Servant.

Discovering

Read Mark 14:12-26.

Exploring

Three scenes are portrayed in this account: the preparation for the Passover, the betrayal by Judas and the Last Supper.

Scene One: Preparation

Mark dates the event "[o]n the first day of Unleavened Bread, when it was customary to sacrifice the paschal lamb" (14:12). His dating is inaccurate since the first day of Unleavened Bread is 15 Nisan; according to the Jewish calendar the lambs were slain on 14 Nisan. His reason for this dating is theological rather than historical. He wishes to connect the meal of Jesus with the Passover meal (14:14) and demonstrate Jesus' foreknowledge of coming events when the disciples "found it just as he had told them" (14:16).

Mark's inaccurate dating of the first day of Unleavened Bread provides additional insight in our study of Scripture. Gospel is faith history rather than profane history. Profane history concerns itself with exact dates and facts, whereas faith history emphasizes a theological explanation. Mark's association of the meal of Jesus with the Passover meal is a theological connection linking Jesus' death with the preparational events for the reader.

Scene Two: The Betrayal

The most difficult passage in the betrayal account appears in 14:21. Was Judas predestined to betray Christ or did he have a choice? The answer is discovered in an understanding of responsibility as demonstrated by Christ in comparison to Judas. Jesus freely accepts the responsibility placed before him by the Scriptures, "The Son of Man is going the way the Scripture tells of him" (14:21). This responsibility will lead him to the cross and death.

Judas is also responsible for his actions. He was given the choice of following Jesus but chose to deny him—a choice which is a different kind of death. Jesus is more pained than condemning of Judas' choice and therefore makes the statement, "It were better for him had he never been born" (14:21).

In the Scriptures, the choice for Christians is clear:

Either we choose God or not, and we are subject to the consequences of the choice. God, the jealous lover, longs for us to choose God. Because God is a lover, however, God never removes the ability to choose. With this understanding of the difference between choice and responsibility as a backdrop, you can now question yourself: "Is it I?"

Scene Three: The Meal

The action surrounding the meal is a symbolic foreshadowing of the future. Just as Jesus took bread and blessed it, broke it and gave it to them, so, too, Jesus will become the bread on Calvary. Just as the bread was broken in order to be shared and therefore unite the disciples into one with Jesus, Jesus offers his body (himself) on Calvary so all might be one with him and with one another in God. This same action was performed in the two feeding stories discussed in Journey 11. Just as the disciples did not understand the loaves of the feeding story, we can assume they do not understand Jesus as bread in this scene.

We see the close connection to the Eucharistic meal celebrated at our Sunday liturgies. In Mark's community and in ours, the bread and wine are offered as the symbols of Jesus' sacrificial death. The Eucharistic meal signifies the messianic banquet of the Kingdom. Just as we sit at the table with God in Eucharist, we will sit at the messianic banquet with God when the Kingdom reaches fulfillment.

The remainder of the Passion narrative is self-explanatory. Only a few comments are needed for clarification:

- The numerous cast of characters within the Passion narrative provides for ample opportunity to employ the mimetic device (see Journey 5). Follow the passion by assuming the roles of Peter, Pilate, Simon or even Jesus. At times in our lives, we find in ourselves aspects of each of the characters. We vacillate between denying Jesus and drawing closer to him.
- Mark 14:51-52 presents the first "streaker" of history. The insertion of this account of the man running away naked has led many people to assume that the man is Mark himself, after the custom of artists who placed themselves in their paintings. It is not meant to be taken literally that Mark was an eyewitness to Jesus' life; rather, he placed himself symbolically within the time frame.

Eugene LaVerdiere, a prominent biblical scholar, believes this naked man symbolizes the disciples of the time. The man flees stripped of all his dignity. His clothing, a linen cloth, reminds us of the baptismal robe. Just as all the disciples have left Jesus, Mark is saying

that the call to discipleship, given in Baptism, is a call to suffering and many will run away. As John in his Gospel associates the Christian with the beloved disciple, Mark associates the difficulty of discipleship with this naked, fleeing, unnamed man.

- The description of Jesus' crowning of thorns (15:16-20), the mockery of the crowd (29-30) and the death itself (33-36) paints an ironic picture of the Messiah now dressed and treated like a common thief. But Jesus has warned of the type of kingdom he will be given on this earth. He has predicted that his crown will be made of thorns, his throne will be the cross and his reign will be one of suffering and death. The same choice given to Jesus and Judas is given to others. Some people choose not to believe in him (15:29). Mark presents to his community (and to us) a Jesus who views from the cross people still waiting for Elijah to come (see Journey 12). Elijah has come, the Messiah is here hanging on the cross, and still some miss the point.
- Previous Journeys have emphasized the importance of the centurion's profession (15:39). As the only human to profess Jesus as the Son of God, the centurion recognizes the true identity of Christ on the cross. Immediately following the centurion's profession is a recognition of the women who have followed Jesus to the cross (15:40-41). Mark leaves the scene with 15:41b: "There were also many others who had come up with him to Jerusalem." One can only wonder whether this statement witnesses to the number in Mark's community who have already experienced suffering and death because of their willingness to profess Jesus as the Son of God.

Looking Back

On Journey 13, you made these discoveries:

- Techniques of "reflective reading for meditation" allow us to pray and write over specific biblical texts.
- Through the anointing by the woman, Jesus instructs us that he is a suffering servant.
- The difference between profane history and faith history is the latter's manipulation of facts and events to provide a *theological* understanding.
- Christians are called to choose God. Each is free in his or her selection but is also responsible for the choice.
- Through the mimetic device we become characters within the Passion. We especially associate ourselves with the man fleeing naked, unwilling to accept the cost of discipleship.
- The centurion's profession can be proclaimed only after witnessing the death of Jesus.

For Further Exploration

Senior, Donald and Eugene LaVerdiere. *The Gospel of Mark*, Audiocassettes. Austin, Texas: Texas Catholic Conference Scripture Seminar, 1984.

Journey 14

Where Is the Ending?

Occasionally a movie's ending will leave us sitting in the dark, both literally and figuratively. When this occurs, we find ourselves rooted in our theater seats, eyes glued to the screen, hoping an additional message will appear. The abruptness of the ending leaves us stunned, for there is something in us that longs for the story to come to a conclusion. An ending simply has to be an ending.

We experience the abrupt ending in Mark (16:8). Although scholars believe 16:8 is the actual ending, my Bible continues with three subheadings: "The Longer Ending," "The Shorter Ending" and the "Freer Logion." These additions attached to Mark's writing hint at the early Church's difficulty with Mark's conclusion. Simply reading these appendages to Mark alerts us to a change in language and style so foreign to his Gospel that most scholars adhere to the theory that the additional endings were added later.

There are three popular interpretations regarding Mark's abrupt ending:

1) While Mark was writing his Gospel, he was arrested for practicing Christianity. Nabbed before completing his Gospel, Mark experienced the same fate he predicted for any disciple of Christ, therefore leaving to other writers the task of completing the Gospel.

2) Since we do not have the original writings of Mark, the ending was lost in translation. When the scribes copying the Gospel realized the ending was lost, they inserted endings of their own.

3) Mark 16:8 is the ending. Mark intended to conclude at this point, believing that he had supplied the reader with a valid ending.

Discovering

Read Mark 16:1-8.

The beginning verses (16:1-4) ring true to our understanding of the Resurrection accounts. The women are going to anoint the body; they are discussing the difficulty of the stone that seals the tomb; and they notice that the stone has been moved when they arrive. Even the day is correct: "When the sabbath was over" (16:1).

Do not be too quick to read through Mark's account in these four verses. If you read the account believing you already are aware of the happenings, you miss the absurdity of the women going to anoint the body. The body already was anointed in 14:3-7 (Journey 13).

Take some time with 14:2: "Very early, just after sunrise,

on the first day of the week...." If you had the luxury of reading Greek and Hebrew, this emphasis on the first day of the week and after sunrise would recall the same language found in the Genesis story of creation. Genesis 1:1-3 reads:

> In the beginning, when God created the heavens and the earth, the earth was a formless wasteland, and darkness covered the abyss, while a mighty wind swept over the waters. Then God said, "Let there be light," and there was light. God saw how good the light was. God then separated the light from the darkness. God called the light "day," and the darkness he called "night." Thus evening came, and morning followed—the first day.

Mark is comparing the "first day of creation" with the "first day of resurrection" for this day in 16:2 is a *new* beginning day of creation.

After the reader is alerted to the "new day of creation," Mark has the women greeted by a man. It is the message of this man which will give credence to Mark's ending at 16:8.

- He tells them not to be amazed (16:6a). If you remember, in Journey 1, we encountered this *amazement* as a key word repeated numerous times in Mark's writing. Throughout Mark's Gospel people are *amazed* at Jesus' healings, exorcism, miracles and at the authority by which he says and does things. Now the women are *amazed* and rightly so. Where they expect to meet death, the women are told of life.
- "You are looking for Jesus of Nazareth..." (16:6b). There is no doubt that he is gone. The same Jesus of Nazareth who was mentioned in other parts of the Gospel (1:9; 1:24; 10:47; 14:67) is no longer trapped in the tomb of death. Again, Mark presents a message of life in a place of death.
- "...who was crucified. He has been raised up; he is not here. See the place where they laid him" (16:6bc). This is the resurrection for Mark. To this tomb was brought Jesus of Nazareth who was executed by the authorities. But "he has been raised up..." and the proof is that the place where they have laid him is empty.

Eugene LaVerdiere provides us with excellent insight concerning this passage. For LaVerdiere, Mark is presenting a clever comparison between three figures:

Jesus at the Transfiguration, the naked man who fled and the messenger in the tomb. The messenger is dressed similarly to Jesus at the Transfiguration. He has on his white robe which now reminds us of Baptism. He is proclaiming the truth about Jesus: Jesus is the Christ who has risen from the dead. This message is at the core of Christian evangelization. This messenger sits amongst death and proclaims life. He is the true disciple.

In contrast, the man who flees naked is stripped of his white cloth and runs away afraid. He fails to see the connection between the Passion and Resurrection and is unable to face the responsibilities of his baptismal promises. We can carry Mark's contrast between these two men one step further. The true follower of Christ must see life amidst all the surrounding signs of death. Remember the chaotic happenings in government and religion which Mark expressed in the apocalyptic style. Now, Mark says that although all things appear bleak, true disciples, like the man in the tomb, sit amidst their dark surroundings and proclaim life.

"Go now and tell his disciples and Peter, 'He is going ahead of you to Galilee, where you will see him just as he told you' "(16:7). The first part of this message tells the women to proclaim the Good News to Jesus' disciples. The second part of the message contains the heart of the account: Jesus is gone ahead to Galilee.

Previous reference was made to the importance of Galilee (see Journey 13). Galilee is more than a geographical place and may be viewed as a multivalent symbol. It is the symbolic place where the *parousia* will come to pass. Jesus' going to Galilee is a symbolic action which assures the reader that the message is to be spread to all of the world. Galilee, unlike Jerusalem, becomes the symbolic place of the Son of Man since Jerusalem symbolizes the place which has fallen under the power of Satan.

Discovering

Read Mark 14:28.

Exploring

What Jesus had predicted in 14:28 has now been accomplished in 16:7. Why should one doubt this since all of Jesus' predictions come true? Did he not predict his Passion three times (see Journey 7)? Did he not predict Peter's denial (14:30)? Therefore, since Jesus predicted he would be in Galilee after he rose from the dead, he must be in Galilee.

The final verse of the Passion narrative (16:8) may be the reason for so much controversy over the ending in

Mark's Gospel. After all, the Lord is risen and there should be joy. Yet "They made their way out and fled from the tomb bewildered and trembling; and because of their great fear, they said nothing to anyone" (16:8).

Scholars have pondered over this verse for centuries since it appears to leave the Gospel in an incomplete state. They do remind us that the incompleteness is not on the part of Christ since he has triumphed on the cross and sits at the right hand of God (14:62). What remains for Christ is to come and gather the faithful (13:27). The incompleteness is on the part of the *community* since the risen Lord continues to be hidden until he comes again. This veil of mystery over the risen Lord along with the women saying nothing recalls the material discussed in Journey 10.

In Journey 10 we read nine different accounts in which people were instructed not to say anything (Messianic secret). This secret is now being revealed since the Resurrection has occurred—not in its entirety, however, since we do not know the day or the hour of Christ's coming. This silence on the part of the women may suggest that the idea of the empty tomb was disclosed at a later time within the early Church. The empty tomb does not appear in any of the early epistle accounts of Paul or other writers. In fact, this account only appears in the Gospels. Despite the uncertainty on the part of scholars regarding Mark's ending, we may gain an understanding of this ending by reflecting on previous Journeys and certain questions.

Mark has taught us that we must move from blindness to sight to insight (see Journey 7). It is important not only that we go to Galilee but also that we gain insight as to what Galilee represents. Perhaps if we begin with some questions regarding ourselves, we will understand this last verse from Mark.

- Are we not a group of people who believe in the Resurrection, proclaim our faith in Christ and yet still have some occasions of disbelief?
- Are there not patterns in our behavior that do not always witness to a risen Christ?
- Are we not longing for something more and believing this "something more" will come at the endtime?
- Finally, do we not believe the Kingdom is here but incomplete until the final coming of Christ?

When will our doubt cease, our behavior be a constant witness to the Resurrection, the Kingdom be perfected? The answer is at the endtime or, in Marcan terms, when we truly *see* Galilee. For it is in Galilee that we gain *insight* into the Son of Man coming in his glory.

We live in the in-between time from the Resurrection to the Second Coming. We are no different than the followers of Jesus or the members of the Marcan community. We wait, and while we wait, we constantly strive to bring about the Good News of Jesus, the Christ, the man from Nazareth. In a sense, we are still bewildered and trembling, and we will totally overcome our fears only when we are with Christ forever.

Looking Back

In Journey 14, you made these discoveries:

- Mark 16:8, although abrupt, is the actual ending of the Gospel.
- There is a close connection between Jesus at the Transfiguration, the man fleeing naked and the man at the tomb. The two men represent types of behavior amongst the followers of Christ: The man at the Passion could not accept the cross. The man at the tomb announces the good news of salvation after the cross.
- The message of the man in the tomb is one of life amidst all signs of death. So, too, although Mark's community lives in the chaotic times of death and persecution, they are to be people of life.
- Galilee symbolically represents the place of Jesus' coming and a sign that the Good News is meant for all peoples.
- The final verse (16:8) portrays the women in the same situation as us. Although the Resurrection has occurred, we live in a time of anticipation waiting for Christ to come again.

For Further Exploration

Senior, Donald and Eugene LaVerdiere. *Gospel of Mark*, Audiocassettes. Austin, Texas: Texas Catholic Conference Scripture Seminar, 1984.

Journey 15

Mark and Beyond

The previous Journeys have allowed you to enter into the specifics of Mark's Gospel. Mark's writings, however, are not mere isolated events but are integral to the entire biblical message. Granted, Mark's suffering servant theme has merit on its own. But you must also witness Mark's message in the context of the entire biblical message.

In some of the Journeys, reference was made to the Hebrew Scriptures. Occasionally, some comparison was given between Mark's writing and either Matthew or Paul. This Journey provides you with the opportunity to take the next step in biblical study by comparing Mark with the other synoptic writers, namely, Matthew and Luke.

The term *synoptics* is a Greek word suggesting that one can place the three Gospels next to one another and generally catch the same material with (*syn*) one look (*optic*). The term *synoptic problem* refers to the difficulty in understanding the relationship between Matthew, Luke and Mark (the Synoptic writers) as well as their distinct differences. The exercises within this Journey introduce a few similarities and differences among the Synoptic Gospels in order to deepen understanding of biblical study. From the study of Mark, you already are aware of some differences between the Synoptic writers:

- Mark does not have an account of the birth of Jesus (referred to as the Infancy Narratives), while Matthew and Luke include accounts of Jesus' birth.
- Mark's Resurrection account is brief and abrupt. Matthew and Luke include appearances of the risen Jesus to various people.

The differences between the Synoptic writers suggest that they are writing to specific communities with specific needs and problems. Witness Mark's need to answer questions from a community which is experiencing persecution and suffering. He answers their questions by presenting Jesus as the suffering Son of God. Matthew and Luke also reveal Jesus as Lord, but a Lord who has meaning to their specific communities.

Although each revelation is presented in a manner respectful of the particular writer's community, it is a revelation for all readers. Thus, the writings of the Synoptic Gospels speak to *a* community and to *all* communities. Mark's writing is relevant to his community and to our communities.

The following exercise provides an opportunity to compare the Synoptic writers. At first glance, the exercise may appear tedious and confusing. A careful execution of the exercises, however, will lead you to a clearer understanding of the similarities and differences of the Gospel accounts.

Discovering

Listed in this exercise are two accounts, the healing of Peter's mother-in-law and John's preaching of repentance. The accounts are listed for you in parallel form with Mark's account presented in the middle of the page, and Matthew on the left and Luke on the right.

Read Mark's account first and then Matthew and Luke. Train your eye to travel over to either Matthew or Luke's account to follow similarities from Mark's writing. Using a pen and ruler, mark the three texts accordingly:

a) If a word is the same in Mark *and* Matthew *or* Luke, underline the word once.

b) If a word is the same in Mark *and* Matthew *and* Luke, underline the word twice.

c) If a word is the same in Matthew *and* Luke *but* not found in Mark, place the word in parentheses.

Healing of Peter's Mother-in-Law

Matthew 8:14-15	Mark 1:29-31	Luke 4:38-39
	Immediately upon leaving the synagogue, he	Leaving the synagogue, he entered the house
Jesus entered Peter's house,	entered the house of Simon and Andrew with James and John.	of Simon.
and found Peter's mother-in-law in bed with a fever.	Simon's mother-in-law lay ill with a fever, and the first thing they did was to tell him about her.	Simon's mother-in-law was in the grip of a severe fever, and they interceded with him for her.
He took her by the hand, and the fever left her.	He went over to her and grasped her hand and helped her up, and the fever left her.	He stood over her and addressed himself to the fever, and it left her.
She got up at once and began to wait on him.	She immediately began to wait on them.	She got up immediately and waited on them.

John's Preaching of Repentance

Here I have included a passage that is found only in Matthew and Luke and not in Mark. Follow the directions for underlining words common to Matthew and Luke only.

Matt. 3:7-10	Luke 3:7-9
When he saw that many of the Pharisees and Sadducees were stepping forward for this bath, he said to them: "You brood of vipers! Who told you to flee from the wrath to come? Give some evidence that you mean to reform. Do not pride yourselves on the claim, 'Abraham is our father.' I tell you, God can raise up children to Abraham from these very stones. Even now the axe is laid to the root of the tree. Every tree that is not fruitful will be cut down and thrown into the fire...."	He would say to the crowds that came out to be baptized by him: "You brood of vipers! Who told you to flee from the wrath to come? Give some evidence that you mean to reform. Do not begin by saying to yourselves, 'Abraham is our father.' I tell you, God can raise up children to Abraham from these stones. Even now the ax is laid to the root of the tree. Every tree that is not fruitful will be cut down and thrown into the fire."

Here is a sample of my underlining of the first account:

Healing of Peter's Mother-in-Law

Matthew 8:14-15	**Mark 1:29-31**	**Luke 4:38-39**
	Immediately upon leaving the synagogue, he entered the house of Simon and Andrew with James and John.	Leaving the synagogue, he entered the house of Simon.
Jesus entered Peter's house,		
and found Peter's mother-in-law in bed with a fever.	Simon's mother-in-law lay ill with a fever, and the first thing they did was to tell him about her.	Simon's mother-in-law was in the grip of a severe fever, and they interceded with him for her.
He took her by the hand, and the fever left her.	He went over to her and grasped her hand and helped her up, and the fever left her.	He stood over her and addressed himself to the fever, and it left her.
She (got up) at once and began to wait on him.	She immediately began to wait on them.	She (got up) immediately and waited on them.

Following is my underlining of the second account:

John's Preaching of Repentance

Matt. 3:7-10	**Luke 3:7-9**
When he saw that many of the Pharisees and Sadducees were stepping forward for this bath, he said to them:	He would say to the crowds that came out to be baptized by him:
("You brood of vipers! Who told you to flee from the wrath to come? Give some evidence that you mean to reform. Do not) pride (yourselves) on the claim, ('Abraham is our father.' I tell you, God can raise up children to Abraham from these) very (stones. Even now the axe is laid to the root of the tree. Every tree that is not fruitful will be cut down and thrown into the fire....")	("You brood of vipers! Who told you to flee from the wrath to come? Give some evidence that you mean to reform. Do not) begin by saying to (yourselves, 'Abraham is our father.' I tell you, God can raise up children to Abraham from these stones. Even now the ax is laid to the root of the tree. Every tree that is not fruitful will be cut down and thrown into the fire.")

Discovering: John's Preaching of Repentance

Notice that all three accounts in the exercise "Healing of Peter's Mother-in-Law," include the word "house" (underlined twice). But only Mark and Luke distinguish it as "Simon's house" (Simon is underlined once since Matthew uses the word "Peter"). The words "got up" are found in both Matthew and Luke but do not appear in Mark's account; therefore, I have placed the words "got up" in parentheses.

In the exercise, "John's Preaching of Repentance," you should notice that the statement placed in quotation marks is almost exactly the same wording in both texts. There are only two differences in these 74 words: Matthew uses the words "pride yourselves on the claim" while Luke writes "begin by saying."

From these two exercises, the following assumptions can be made:

- Matthew and Luke had a common source that they both used in writing their Gospel. If you look again at the account of "John's Preaching of Repentance," 69 of the 74 words are exactly the same. This is certainly more than coincidental. Any teacher receiving such exact copies from several students would certainly accuse the writers of plagiarism. From this example, and many others within Luke and Matthew, it is believed that both writers had a common source containing sayings of Jesus. This common source inserted into Matthew and Luke's Gospels is referred to as the "Q-Source." The title refers to an unknown source; "Q" stands for the German *quelle* meaning "source."
- Mark either did not have the Q-Source, since these sayings of Jesus do not appear in his writings, or he chose not to use it. Some scholars believe the former conjecture is more likely.
- In some accounts (an example being the healing of Peter's mother-in-law), there are great similarities among all three writers. Using this type of comparison, scholars conclude that Mark was the first Gospel writer and Matthew and Luke copied portions of his Gospel into their writings. Scholars date Mark's writing around A.D. 70, a point observed in Journey 12. The dating of Matthew and Luke is approximately 10 years later, A.D. 80.
- Scholars also assume that Matthew and Luke had materials of their own which only appear in each particular Gospel. An example of this is found in Luke 15, the story of the Prodigal Son. Although a popular scriptural piece, the account is only found in Luke. This point is worth noting, although the exercises you just completed do not list passages found exclusively in either Mark, Matthew or Luke.

The assumptions presented in the preceding paragraphs allow scholars to construct some ideas about the formulation of the Gospels. Remember that present modern-day devices (tape recorders and video machines) were not available to first-century Christians. If Mark's writing did not begin until around A.D. 70, this was 30 or 40 years after the death of Jesus.

From your study of Mark 13 (Journey 12), you saw that the early Christians believed Christ's second coming would happen within their lifetime. Tradition mentions that the early Christian communities gathered together to tell the story of Jesus in order to obtain converts and deepen their own faith. The events that lead to the written Gospel message stretch from the telling of the story of Jesus to the writing of the story of Jesus, in other words,

from the oral tradition to the written tradition. As we saw in Journey 4, this transition developed in three levels:

- what Jesus actually said;
- what the disciples preached about Jesus and his sayings;
- what the writers wrote about what Jesus said.

Realizing that the development of the Gospel stretches from the actual sayings of Jesus to the writing of these sayings of Jesus, the following diagram demonstrates how the writers acquired the material for their Gospels.

An explanation of the two-source theory is:

- Mark had his own source (the Q-Source) while writing his Gospel.
- Matthew borrowed from both Mark and the Q-Source and also had materials of his own.
- Luke borrowed from both Mark and the Q-Source and also had materials of his own.

Given the work performed in this Journey, you may be wondering about the inspiration of the Gospel message. Is it inspired by God, or is it one writer copying from another?

The term *inspired* means God is definitely the author of the Bible. God, as the principal author, used individuals as the human authors to have the Scriptures teach firmly, faithfully and without error that truth which God wanted written for the sake of our salvation. God incited the writer to write and assisted the writer correctly to conceive all that God intended. The message of the Bible is one of *truth* since God, as the principal author, *is* truth. Mark presents the truth of God but not the *complete* truth, since the other Gospels and epistles present much more. Even the whole Bible does not give the *complete* truth, for God cannot be captured in human language.

In Mark's Gospel the *truth* is found in Christ, who is the suffering servant Son of God. This is the reason Mark elaborates on Peter's profession found in 8:29. Merely stopping at this passage would claim Christ to be only a miracle-worker. This is not the *truth* of God. Rather, the profession of Peter is complete when joined with the profession of the centurion (15:39), who claims Christ as the Son of God after understanding the cross. Mark, as the human author, presents the complete truth of God, the principal author, because the text is inspired by God and can only proclaim *truth*.

God, however, did not remove the natural ability of the writer to think and act. The writer is not merely a puppet for God but is free. Yet, if the writer retains human freedom, can we state the Bible is inerrant? The inerrancy is rooted in the authorship by God who is all *truth*. This does not mean that the Bible is without error; it is, however, without error in the essential message from God.

The authors, human and fallible, did insert their own personal opinions, but these opinions do not affect the truth of the message. Remember Mark's strong belief that Jesus is coming in his lifetime and his incorrect dating of the Preparation Day for Passover. Mark obviously does not know when the end will come, but he does know the dating of the Preparation Day for Passover. In Journey 13 remember we discovered that his dating is theological rather than historical.

The writers possess an "eastern" mentality rather than a "western" mentality. Thus, our western understanding of logic cannot be applied to them. The writer is human and therefore expresses the message in human terms, thus limiting it to particular forms of prose and poetry. The limitation to particular forms of writing, however, does not in itself prove the message false. No matter what style the writer employs or what opinions the writer inserts, the essential message is inspired by God as an affirmation of the very truth leading to salvation.

Finally, we must recognize that the author does not work in a vacuum. Granted the author is inspired–but inspired as a member of a community. The writer derives the message from people of the past who told the story of Jesus and continues to be nourished in this story by the present community. As part of a community, the author sometimes challenges, encourages, comforts and expresses the community's faith. This is not an individual expression of faith, but a community's expression of faith. It is from this understanding of faith–which is an experience of God–that I define the Bible as a book of faith, written by people of faith to a community of faith.

Looking Back

In Journey 15 you made these discoveries:

- The synoptic Gospels were written by Matthew, Mark and Luke. Although we may place these Gospels side by side, each Gospel is shaped by the author's revelation of who Jesus is and by the community.
- The technique of underlining reveals a two-source theory in that Matthew and Luke had copies of Mark's Gospel, sayings of Jesus entitled the Q-Source and their

own materials. Scholars believe that Mark wrote first (A.D. 70) and was followed approximately 10 years later by Matthew and Luke.
- The Bible is inspired; God is its author. God, however, does not use the human author as a puppet but rather graces the author to reveal something true about God.
- Despite the fallibility of the author, which is displayed by personal opinion and beliefs, the Bible is inerrant. In that it never detours from the essential message of salvation.

For Further Exploration

Perrin, Norman. *The New Testament: An Introduction.* New York: Harcourt Brace Jovanovich, Inc., 1974.

Smith, Richard. "Inspiration and Inerrancy." *Jerome Biblical Commentary*, ed. Raymond E. Brown, et al., Vol. I. Englewood Cliffs, N.J.: Prentice-Hall, 1969.

Spivey, Robert and D. Moody Smith. *Anatomy of the New Testament: A Guide to Its Structure and Meaning*, 3rd ed. New York: Macmillan Publishing Co., 1982.

Throckmorton, Burton H. *Gospel Parallels*, 4th ed. Nashville/New York: Nelson Publishing Co., 1979.

Journey 16

The Ending and the Beginning

Journeys never really end. We arrive at an understanding only to realize there is more to comprehend. We have spent our time studying Mark's Gospel only to realize that there is more to study. These 16 Journeys provide a beginning, and from this beginning we continue our Journey into the Gospel and with Christ.

Our constant hunger for the Word is actually what Mark is presenting in his entire Gospel; it is found clearly in its final verses (Journey 14). In Mark 16:8, we are left with women in fear and trembling. Mark does not present postresurrection appearances, as do Matthew and Luke. For him, the postresurrection accounts are found in reading the entire Gospel. What we profess in 1:1 is affirmed throughout Mark's Gospel and by all people of the Word. Our reading of Mark is a challenge to make Christ present *here*—in our own lives. We do not read Mark's account as some historical document of the past but as a living Word made present by our witness to the Suffering Servant Christ. If we understand the true cost of discipleship and the challenge of the cross, we can attest to this being the Gospel of Jesus Christ, the Son of God.

Therefore, the final Journey challenges you to return to where you began. In this Journey you are asked to reread Mark in one sitting, just as you did in Journey 1. The beauty of the Gospel, as well as its challenge, is that you must always hear the Word anew. Each time you enter into the Gospel you listen to its message as if it were the first time.

Now you are aware of some ideas found within Mark's writing. You have discovered key words and ideas. You have investigated key passages and titles. You have reflected on the meaning of Mark's message by placing yourself within certain scenes. You have viewed references from the Hebrew Scriptures as foundations to Mark's understanding. You have familiarized yourself with the cultural and historical milieu of Mark's time. You have employed some of the tools of biblical criticism.

All of this awareness will have little effect unless you allow Mark's message to transform your mind and heart. In rereading Mark you are asked to proclaim again: "Jesus is the Son of God!"

Discovering

Read Mark's Gospel.

On completing the reading of Mark's Gospel, write your understanding of Mark's message. The space provided is for your reflection.

Looking Back

In Journey 16, you made these discoveries:

- In lieu of postresurrection accounts of Jesus' appearances, Mark offers his entire Gospel as the story of the postresurrection Jesus. This absence of postresurrection accounts is a challenge to us to make the Gospel present in our own lives and in the life of our community.
- We always must read the Gospel as if for the first time.
- All the discoveries made in these Journeys have no meaning unless the Gospel message transforms our minds and hearts.

For Further Exploration

To continue your journey with the Gospel of Mark, see the annotated bibliography provided on p. 59.

Annotated Bibliography

Anderson, Bernhard. *Understanding the Old Testament*, 4th ed. Englewood Cliffs, N.J.: Prentice Hall, 1986.

This textbook is a popular resource for survey courses in the Hebrew Scriptures on the undergraduate and graduate level. It provides an excellent foundation for understanding the Old Testament. With a solid background in the Old Testament, the student will grow to appreciate the writings of the New Testament.

Flanagan, Neil. *Mark, Matthew, and Luke: A Guide to the Gospel Parallels*. Collegeville, Minn.: The Liturgical Press, 1978.

In this guide to Burton Throckmorton's text, *Gospel Parallels*, Flanagan shares classroom notes from his teaching courses. His section on Mark's Gospel provides an excellent background to the structure of Mark, and the prediction, misunderstanding and teaching sections found in the Gospel. Flanagan also provides material concerning the time, place and author of the Gospel, as well as information concerning the Q-Source.

Fuller, Reginald. *The Gospel of Mark*, audiocassettes. Kansas City: National Catholic Reporter Publishing Co.

This series on Mark is a set of eight tapes (no longer in print) by a noted Anglican scholar. Fuller presents a detailed exegesis of Mark's writing, as well as background information to the time, place and author of the Gospel. A masterful teacher, Fuller writes with a style suitable for both the beginning and advanced biblical scholar. Of special note is his presentation on evil spirits, the Marcan sandwich and the two blind men's stories.

Hanson, James. *If I'm a Christian, Why Be a Catholic?: The Biblical Roots of Catholic Faith*. Ramsey, N.J.: Paulist Press, 1984.

Hanson moves us beyond just Mark's Gospel to an overview of Catholic thought and its biblical foundation. This text is an excellent resource for discussion and prayer for any individual interested in tracing Catholic beliefs to their biblical roots.

Harrington, Wilfrid. *Mark*. New Testament Message, Vol. 4. Wilmington, Del.: Michael Glazier, Inc., 1979.

Part of an entire commentary on the Christian Scriptures, this book presents a portion of the scriptural account (a *pericope*) and then a commentary on the account. This source would be an excellent supplementary guide for people desiring more information on any Journey presented in the manual.

Harrington details the structure for the Marcan sandwich on pp. 43-48. This source also provides information on passages not discussed in this manual.

Jerome Biblical Commentary, ed. Raymond E. Brown, et al. Englewood Cliffs, N.J.: Prentice Hall, 1969.

A major resource for biblical study, this commentary provides explanations of biblical matter in both the Hebrew Scriptures and Christian Scriptures. Besides the recommended articles on "Inspiration and Inerrancy" by Richard Smith, the reader will discover an entire section dedicated to an explanation of Mark's Gospel. It should be noted that the editors of this commentary, Raymond Brown, Joseph Fitzmyer and Roland Murphy, are considered the leading Catholic biblical scholars of our time.

Jewett, Robert. *Jesus Against the Rapture*. Philadelphia: Westminster Press, 1979.

Robert Jewett selects seven popular Scripture passages which he believes are misinterpreted by popular writers of an evangelical mode. Although not all seven passages are from Mark, his work on Mark 13, "Only the Abba Knows," is worthwhile reading. This text is an excellent source for Christians who follow a more orthodox view of Scripture study than the fundamentalist view.

Kee, Howard Clark. *Community of a New Age: Studies in Mark's Gospel*. Philadelphia: Westminster Press, 1977.

This work provides a background to the Marcan community. Kee lays claim to Mark's community as the formation of a new covenant and an eschatological witness to the world. Of special note is his explanation of Mark's community breaking from family blood ties to form new relationships with brothers and sisters of faith. Once Kee establishes this foundation, he details the rules, structure and life of the Marcan community. His approach moves away from the typical historical model to insights presented in a sociological method.

Kelber, Werner H. *Mark's Story of Jesus*. Philadelphia: Fortress Press, 1979.

Kelber provides an interesting style of commentary on Mark's Gospel. Without inserting the actual scriptural passages, he weaves the accounts of Mark's writing into a narrative form which reads like a novel. It is Kelber's information concerning the hidden revelation at the baptism that is found in this manual. Kelber divides Mark into five main parts and supplies an excellent summary at the end of each of his sections.

Kingsbury, Jack Dean. *The Christology of Mark's Gospel.* Philadelphia: Fortress Press, 1983.

Beginning with an investigation of William Wrede's work on the messianic secret in Mark, Kingsbury critiques the major theological positions concerning Mark's titles for Jesus. Although Kingsbury discusses these titles, he centers on Son of God and Son of Man as the primary titles of the Gospel. For Kingsbury, the Son of Man title is one of majesty and not necessarily a title specifying "who Jesus is." Kingsbury also claims that Mark is indeed the one who understands the true identity of Jesus and presents this image to his community.

LaVerdiere, Eugene. *The Gospel of Mark,* 4 half-hour video programs. Produced by Dominican Central Productions, 1909 South Ashland Ave., Chicago, Ill. 60608, 1986.

Presented in dialogue form as a discussion between Father LaVerdiere and Father Peter J. Hereley, these videos provide an excellent overview of the Gospel of Mark. Of special note is Video Two, "You Give Them to Eat," in which LaVerdiere demonstrates the importance of feeding stories with Psalm 23. The linkage between the desert place of the feeding stories and the green pastures of the psalm is an interesting balance between the Hebrew and Christian Scriptures.

O'Grady, John. *Mark: The Sorrowful Gospel.* Ramsey, N.J.: Paulist Press, 1981.

Centering on Mark's Christology, O'Grady leads the reader from the beginning faith of the Christian community to the faith presented in Gospel form. One of the many major advantages of this text is O'Grady's "Selected Bibliography" printed at the end of his book. There he lists and summarizes 28 sources on Mark's Gospel.

Perkins, Pheme. *Reading the New Testament: An Introduction,* 2nd ed. Ramsey, N.J.: Paulist Press, 1988.

Perkins' second edition of her work, originally published in 1978, provides an excellent introduction to biblical study. Her first four chapters provide a clear understanding of general biblical study, as well as the world and life of Jesus. A chapter on Mark's Gospel presents a broad overview of some material presented in this manual.

Perrin, Norman. *Jesus and the Language of the Kingdom: Symbol and Metaphor in New Testament Interpretation.* Philadelphia: Fortress Press, 1976.

Although this source deals with a focused view on the Kingdom from all of Scripture, Perrin gives some interesting background to the Kingdom parables found in Mark 13. This text also supplies further insight concerning the seed parables of Mark 4, which are not highlighted in this manual.

Rhoads, David and Donald Michie. *Mark As Story: An Introduction to the Narrative of a Gospel.* Philadelphia: Fortress Press, 1982.

A combined effort by a literary scholar (Michie) and a biblical scholar (Rhoads), this text gives an in-depth view to Scripture as narrative. Rhoads and Michie present Mark's Gospel in the beginning of their book without chapter and verse designations, thereby allowing the reader to view the piece as a story. The remainder of their work comments on the various characteristics affecting the narrative: style, characters, plot and narrator. This text provides background information about Mark as the omniscient narrator, that is, as one who has unlimited knowledge in order to tell the complete story.

Senior, Donald and Eugene LaVerdiere. *The Gospel of Mark,* Audiocassettes. Produced by Texas Catholic Conference Scripture Seminar, St. Edward's University, 3001 S. Congress, Austin, Texas 78704, October 14-17, 1984.

These audiocassettes were produced from a three-day conference on Mark's Gospel for people in the dioceses of Texas. Donald Senior begins the series and presents interesting information concerning contemporary discoveries about Galilee. LaVerdiere covers the latter parts of Mark's Gospel and presents his recent discoveries of the linkage connecting the linen cloth of the Transfiguration, the man fleeing naked and the messenger in the tomb.

Spivey, Robert and D. Moody Smith. *Anatomy of the New Testament: Its Structure and Meaning.* New York: Macmillan Publishing Co, Inc., 1982.

This source is basically a textbook for undergraduate courses on the Christian Scriptures. Although the text provides information on all of the Christian Scriptures, Chapter Two deals specifically with Mark's Gospel. The text provides excellent background information on the suffering servant theme of Mark.